Culture, Politics,
and Irish School Dropouts

Critical Studies in Education and Culture Series

Culture, Politics, and Irish School Dropouts

Constructing Political Identities

G. Honor Fagan

Critical Studies in Education and Culture Series
Edited by Henry A. Giroux and Paulo Freire

Bergin & Garvey
Westport, Connecticut • London

Library of Congress Cataloging-in-Publication Data

Fagan, G. Honor.
    Culture, politics, and Irish school dropouts : constructing
political identities / G. Honor Fagan.
        p. cm. — (Critical studies in education and culture series,
    ISSN 1064–8615)
    Includes bibliographical references and index.
    ISBN 0–89789–439–1 (alk. paper)
        1. School dropouts—Ireland—Attitudes. 2. School dropouts—
Ireland—Interviews. 3. Group identity—Ireland. 4. Politics and
education—Ireland. 5. Education—Social aspects—Ireland.
I. Title. II. Series.
LC145.I73F34 1995
371.2'913'09417—dc20   95–6949

British Library Cataloguing in Publication Data is available.

Library of Congress Catalog Card Number: 95–6949

ISBN: 0–89789–439–1
ISSN: 1064–8615

First published in 1995

Bergin & Garvey, 88 Post Road West, Westport, CT 06881
An imprint of Greenwood Publishing Group, Inc.

Printed in the United States of America

The paper used in this book complies with the
Permanent Paper Standard issued by the National
Information Standards Organization (Z39.48–1984).

10 9 8 7 6 5 4 3 2 1

CONTENTS

SERIES FOREWORD

One of the central characteristics of radical social theories within the last decade has been a move away from the singularity of class or gender as a defining principle of identity and political struggle. In part, such a theoretical move has opened up the possibility for recognizing the multiple subject positions that constitute any claim to identity. In more specific terms, it has meant recognizing the complex ways in which identities are formed, lived out, and reconstructed. It has also brought about a renewed interest in addressing how domination, accommodation, and resistance works itself out within specific institutional and cultural sites. Similarly, the pluralization of identity has generated a renewed interest in the importance of a discourse of critical agency and a renewed hope in constructing energized social movements based on democratic models of struggle.

It is worth noting that the field of critical education has a distinguished history of remarkable ethnographic studies that explore how student identities are constructed within the often repressive atmosphere of schools. But most of the theoretical work done in this field bears the weight of a historical time in which domination either appears to close off the possibility for active social change or is defined so narrowly that it unconsciously reproduces its own brand of racist and sexist discrimination. Even where such studies became more inclusive around issues of class, race, and gender, they suffered from a refusal to link complex representations of identity formation to broader considerations of how to reconstruct public life as part of a radical democratic project. Too much of this work—in its attempt to provide access to the voices of subordinate groups of students—validated such voices, and experiences were either constructed or might be critically engaged. Experience appeared, in these studies, to guarantee its own politics as well as a particular species of anti-intellectualization.

Honor Fagan has written a remarkable book in which she builds upon the radical traditions of schooling while simultaneously challenging and moving beyond their theoretical and political shortcomings. While Fagan's work centers around an investigation of early school-leavers in Ireland, she is not content to mimic the discourse of reproduction and resistance. On the contrary, she is primarily concerned with how the construction of student identities within an educational setting provides political and pedagogical insights into the dynamics of critical human agency, transformative pedagogy, and the reconstruction of democratic life. Linking narratives of struggle to a relationship between social empowerment and democratic struggle, Fagan draws upon the work of a number of poststructuralist theorists who address language as a defining principle of politics and social change. Fagan not only expands this theoretical work, she gives it a practical application in her attempt to deepen the political nature of pedagogy by making discourse central to the construction of identity and indispensable for constructing a politics of hope and possibility. Rejecting the opposition between theorist and activist, she redefines the role of the educator as a public intellectual and in so doing provides new theoretical ground for educators to take a stand without standing still, to engage in a political project without imposing a political agenda upon their students.

Fagan makes language a site of imagination and resistance, but in doing so she reconfigures the intersection of pedagogy and commitment as an in-between zone, a space in which the relevance of what it means to be an educator becomes synonymous with being critical, provocative, and transformative. For Fagan, to be an educator or cultural worker means being an activist intellectual located within a critical discourse committed to forms of cultural production that open up strategies to transform the present and future for those students whose survival and growth is central to the very meaning of democratic life.

Fagan's study offers educators the opportunity to recognize that the moral content of one's identity is inexorably linked to how one addresses issues that either close down or open up the possibility of democratic public life. Clearly, this would suggest a renewed importance in how power is centered or decentered in educational sites, how language works to expand the capacity to think and act critically, and how resources are used to limit or expand the possibility for cultural and political democracy. Moreover, Fagan's political and ethnographic study provides North American educators and others with the opportunity to forge transnational solidarities that link diverse pedagogical and political studies around a notion of radical democracy that makes difference a defining principle of public culture.

HENRY A. GIROUX

Culture, Politics, and Irish School Dropouts

Introduction

This book paints a picture of the struggle, the everyday lives, and the cultural identities of early school-leavers. Its purpose is to draw up a political practice, a cultural politics, that relates to the particular position of early school-leavers. This political practice is theorized within a poststructuralist and post-Marxist framework.

Sociological theories of education have addressed the question of early school-leaving as a political problem since the early 1970s, in particular through the reproduction/resistance debate. Theorists interested in linking education to politics turned to Marxism, which was seen as the main critical theory available to academics, and this in turn gave rise to explanations in terms of reproduction. The argument was that the forces of (re)production, within a capitalist system, determine the school failure of those from lower socioeconomic backgrounds in order to reproduce the class system and the capitalist mode of production. Thus, early school-leaving was determined by the capitalist system. Arising from a critique of the determinism of the reproduction model, the late 1970s saw the emergence of a more voluntarist Marxist approach to early school-leaving, namely the "resistance perspective." Resistance theory, while accepting the basic merits of the reproduction perspective, concentrated more on active working-class participation in dropping out of school. The argument was that working-class underachievement was due to political resistance on the part of the working class and to their educational suppression, and so it marks a first attempt by a Marxist analysis to take up power more dialectically.

From the 1970s onwards, other perspectives splintered the Marxist narrative on educational disadvantage. A new critical focus on gender and race strengthened and expanded the debate on educational disadvantage. It was no longer enough to examine school dropouts in the simple light of class reproduction as race and gender perspectives were brought to bear. Academic work began to center around identifying the dominant ideological interests that serve class, gender, and race oppression[1] in schools. The educational underachievement of all oppressed groups was clearly articulated as a political problem. Today, a genuine intellectual initiative can be successfully mounted to unravel the political and economic injustices within education.

Building on this initiative, and the indisputable recognition that early school-leaving is a political issue, this book represents an attempt to move the political debate and practice forward. While acknowledging that unraveling and identifying economic injustices and ideological interests associated with early school-leaving are extremely important political moments, there are other aspects of political struggle. A major theme of this book is the primacy of politics, and of democratic political practice in particular. I attempt a theoretical and practical movement, from critically analyzing early school-leaving as a social and political reality to constructing and representing early school-leavers as potential agents of radical democratic politics. In this way I wish to point to the value of discursively creating a new and empowering political space for early school-leavers.

The possibility of formulating this new trajectory for early school-leavers rests on insights gleaned from the progressive theoretical paradigms of the late 1980s and 1990s such as poststructuralism, postmodernism, feminism, postcolonialism, post-Marxism, and critical cultural studies. The insights of these theoretical movements are of crucial importance to the development of new political spaces for the underprivileged. In referring to the political importance of theory in another context, Homi Bhabha (1988) argues that, collectively, these theoretical paradigms extend the domain of politics beyond a strategy dominated by the forces of economic and social control. This book investigates the prospects for a political strategy for early school-leavers which goes beyond a critique of these forces of social and economic control.

Alongside the emergence of these new theoretical problematics we have witnessed the emergence of a new progressive or transformative cultural politics. Proponents of this, heavily influenced by the wave of poststructuralism, have sought to intervene in their fields to help create the conditions for the emergence of what Homi Bhabha refers to as a "socialist *community* of interest and articulation" (1988). Such politics seeks to forge links between specific or site-based discourses and the broader field that Laclau and Mouffe refer to as a socialist strategy for radical democratic politics (1985). The linkage I pursue in this book is that between the particular site of early school-leavers, their everyday lives and identities, and the broader discourse of radical democracy. I argue that the discourse of radical democracy or of a "socialist community of interest and articulation" would articulate the social relations of early school-leaving as oppressive. It can, furthermore, act as an external referent against which the specifics of a new space for early school-leavers can be struggled for and articulated.

Situating itself within cultural politics, this work focuses on a central theoretical and political insight—namely, the specific value of a politics of cultural production insofar as it holds transformative possibilities. This cultural politics has a dual focus: the will to break down the current material space allocated to, and produced for, early school-leavers; and the will to overcome the absence of a discursive political formation that would best represent the interests of early school-leavers. More specifically, it is about creating, theorizing, and drawing up a cultural politics of early school-leaving with/for early school-leavers, and for cultural workers who struggle alongside early school-leavers. This cultural politics is theorized in such a way that, while it deals with the specifics of the material and political space of early school-leavers, it simultaneously draws from and contributes to the broader politics of radical democracy.

I argue that the development of this cultural politics necessitates a theoretical move beyond a structuralist framework to a post-structuralist one. From a poststructuralist perspective, even a critical social theory such as structuralism is simply a discourse of critique. I maintain that we need to develop a language of reconstruction, transformation, and possibility. To tackle the issue of early school-leaving in the 1990s, we require strategies that take account of the poststructuralist analysis of the *discursive* construction of power relations and their dynamics. Discourse is a central poststructuralist concept that refers to what gets talked about or said, although, within a poststructuralist framework, this is not separable from the practices described. Discourse, from this perspective, describes, informs, and constitutes practices. It is not separable from people's "reality," since subjectivies are in fact constituted through discourse, nor is it in a relation of exteriority with respect to the material. From this perspective, discourse is constitutive of the "real world" of early school-leavers, and the material aspects of their lives bears a direct relation to its discursive construction.

It is only with this poststructuralist understanding of discursive construction of power relations that this book can attempt to play a role in a wider political struggle. My role is the writing of a text, but a text embodied in practice. Those readers who believe in the simple binary oppositions of the "theorist" and the "activist" will be frustrated with, and skeptical of, this project. To counteract this frustration, I urge the reader to be open to the possibility of political writing where the intellectual and the activist are not seen in opposition to each other, but rather complementary. This book is committed equally to these two dimensions of the political struggle for transformation.

This book is set in the context of the Republic of Ireland, where early school-leaving has been seen to be a problem since the 1970s. The revolutionary impetus of the struggle for independence ensured a rhetoric of equal rights for all, which took very seriously the role education could play in achieving a better way of life for the Irish people. The educational system was set up along strict meritocratic guidelines, and for a long time the situation remained unquestioned, the new system being at least more democratic than the old colonial one. In the last ten to twenty years the educational system has been questioned as to its democratic claims compared to the reality it delivers. The extent of educational "disadvantage," while no worse, and in fact better, than that in many Western countries, has been the focus of social research[2] that shows that early school-leaving and educational "disadvantage" is seen as a problem, in that it represents a failure on the part of the Irish State to serve all its citizens equally.

The 1980s saw considerable public attention being paid to unemployment and emigration. Government attention focused on youth unemployment, and the connection between unemployment and early school-leaving was examined. A tax (a youth employment levy) was raised to fund a government scheme (A Social Guarantee for Young People), which "guaranteed" that the government would cut down youth unemployment. This would be done by "employing" young people on government "transition" schemes—programs of work to help young people make the transition from school to work.[3] The government's response to the articulation of early school-leaving as a problem in terms of unemployment led to a missed political opportunity and worked to the detriment of long-term equity objectives. The government responded to public concern in the short term, but only postponed the problem by shunting it into sinister and manipulative programs—sinister because young unemployed people have little choice as to whether or not they go on the schemes, and manipulative in that they deliberately create a non-unionized, unprotected form of underpaid labor. It is in this social context that the dialogues with the early school-leavers presented in Part I take place. The early school-leavers speaking out in the following pages attended one of these government training programs, namely a Community Training Workshop. They live in an inner-city council estate and, having left school early, find themselves hopelessly unemployed and struggling to gain the basic education and income that the State is supposed to provide for all its citizens.

This book is organized into three sections. Part I presents conversations, structured by me, with early school-leavers. These conversations were organized around three questions: how do early school-leavers represent their experience of schooling, of school leaving in retrospect, and of their current and future material and social situations? My presentation of these conversations is structured around images of these young people as I see them, as subjectivities and identities in a cultural process of construction. The script of the dialogues presents the young people historicizing their own past experiences and analyzing their current and future work prospects. In the text I concurrently narrate and summarize these conversations.

In Part II, I argue that early school-leavers occupy a subordinate position in terms of material location and show how "objective" academic discourses have contributed to establishing the underpinning relations of subordination. I explore the sociological theories of reproduction and resistance and carry out a reproductionist/ resistance reading of the representations of the early school-leaver's life experiences as presented in Part I. I then proceed to analyze the theoretical and political contribution these perspectives can make to the problem of early school-leaving. I do this to present the reader with a sense both of the progress made in solving the problem through critical analysis and of the limitations of simply viewing the problem within the framework of these perspectives.

Part III constructs a discourse of social change, but without transcending the realities of the everyday lives and struggles of the early school-leavers as they encounter them. It conceptualizes early school-leaving as representing a political crisis of space and the struggle of school-leavers as democratic. New languages and new theories are introduced which move the issue into the realm of transformative politics. I outline strategies for a cultural politics of relevance to early school-leaving. I examine the broad theoretical domain of radical democracy and cultural studies in order to conceptualize this politics. I conclude by drawing up elements of a cultural, political, and educational strategy for work with, by, and for early school-leavers.

NOTES

1. For examples of work on gender oppression in Ireland, see M. Cullen (ed.), *Girls Don't Do Honours—Irish Women in Education in the 19th and 20th Centuries* (Dublin: Women's Education Bureau, 1987); in Britain on resistance and gender, see A. McRobbie & J. Garber, "Girls and Subcultures," in *Resistance through Ritual*, edited by S. Hall & T. Jefferson (London: Hutchinson,

1976); and on race, see Kum-Kum Bhavnani's *Talking Politics* (Cambridge: Cambridge University Press, 1991).

2. For social research of this nature, see R. Breen, *Education and the Labour Market: Work and Unemployment among Recent Cohorts of Irish School-Leavers* (Dublin: Economic and Social Research Institute, Paper 119, 1984a); R. Breen, "Status Attainment or Job Attainment? The Effects of Sex and Class on Youth Unemployment," *British Journal of Sociology.* *35* (No. 3, 1984b), 363–386; R. Breen, B. Whelan, & J. Costigan, "School Leavers 1980–1986. A Report to the Department of Labour" (Dublin: Economic and Social Research Institute, 1986); D. Hannan et al., *Schooling and Sex-Roles: Sex Difference and Student Choice in Irish Post-Primary Schools* (Dublin: Economic and Social Research Institute, Paper No. 113, 1983); and J. J. Sexton, *Transition from School to Work and Early Labour Market Experience* (Dublin: Economic and Social Research Institute, Paper No. 141, 1988).

3. For an example of social research on government policy, see R. Breen, *Education, Employment and Training in the Youth Labour Market* (Dublin: Economic and Social Research Institute, 1991). For an example of a critical cultural approach to these transition schemes in the British context, see R. Hollands, *The Long Transition: Class, Culture, and Youth Training* (London: Macmillan Education, 1990).

PART I

IDENTITIES-IN-CULTURE: CONVERSATIONS WITH EARLY SCHOOL-LEAVERS

A necessary element for constructing a political practice around early school-leaving is a grounding in the material terrain that early school-leavers occupy. This involves highlighting their struggle in terms of acknowledging the specificity of their demands, their concrete resistances, and their efforts towards a public sphere of influence. There are many practical ways of achieving this grounding, but the following is a reading of some conversations I held with a group of early school-leavers which I see as providing a text that would give some indication of the subjectivities, identities, struggles, and articulations of early school-leavers.

I reject the notion of speaking for early school-leavers, and the commentary is quite clearly about my interpretation of what they say. I am interpreting what they say to me, and therefore this is as much about me as about them. In constructing these conversations with the young people, a textual picture of the political and material location of early school-leavers is provided. When entering into these conversations, I wanted to find out what the young people had to say about their circumstances and their everyday life and how they would discursively construct their identities. In a specific time, in a specific place, this is what specific young early school-leavers told me and what I asked them. In terms of the project of this book, this presentation has a dual role—from a cultural point of view, this provides me with a text from which there is a possibility of glimpsing or pursuing momentary "identities-in-culture."[1] From a political perspective, this text provides one starting point from which to theorize a specific cultural politics that addresses early school-leavers.

The following is a record of "conversations with a purpose"[2] and my commentary on these conversations. The early school-leavers involved live in an urban lower-socioeconomic-status area in Dublin, Ireland. I have organized the discussions into three different sections: their views on school, early school-leaving, and their current work or unemployment situation. I present them here in order to provide a constructed text of three dimensions of their lived experiences.

NOTES

1. See A. McRobbie's call for a methodology, for a new paradigm for conceptualizing "identity-in-culture": "Post-Marxism and Cultural Studies: A Postscript," in *Cultural Studies* (New York: Routledge, 1992, pp. 719–731).

2. Kum-Kum Bhavnani uses this terminology to describe a politically concerned type of interviewing methodology in her book, *Talking Politics* (Cambridge: Cambridge University Press, 1991).

1

Schooling

The early school-leavers' relationship with schooling was, in its mildest form, an unhealthy one. Uneasy cooperation between the two developed into the complete rejection of one by the other. In order to trace this rejection of schooling, or the rejection by the school system of these particular young people, it is necessary to relate their account of schooling. This section describes the early school-leavers' attitudes to school and their perspective on the curriculum and on the teachers. This is followed by an outline of their responses to schooling. Finally, occasions of direct conflict between the young people and the schooling system are described.

OVERALL ATTITUDE TO SCHOOLING

The young people's attitude to their schooling ranged from tolerance to extreme dislike. The vast majority conveyed a very definite dislike for school.

Honor Fagan [henceforth HF]: Did you hate it or just not like it?
Kevin: Just hated it, despised it.

or

Cyril: Fucking hated it.
Dave: Brutal, hated it.

Others elaborated more on their dislike.

Liam: No, I didn't like it at all.
HF: What was wrong with it?
Liam: What was right with it! It was just boring, writing and doing
   exams and all that stuff, you know.

Their boredom is connected with their lack of interest.

Judy: I didn't really like school, I wasn't interested in it. You know,
   like, it wasn't interesting enough sitting down doing your work, all
   the time doing what you're told. It wasn't any fun.

Through contact with the young people, it became apparent that
the only two who had said they liked school were two young
women who had been expelled, or "thrown out" of school. Both
wanted to go back to school, to make a fresh start, but on their own
terms.

The fact that young people express a dislike for school is not in
itself unusual, but the fact that so many express extreme dislike, in
retrospect, is notable. When describing more specifically what
they disliked about school, they focused on the curriculum, on the
teaching process, and on the teachers.

PERSPECTIVE ON THE CURRICULUM

Sometimes a particular subject was the object of the dislike.

HF: What did you hate most about it?
Mairead: Math. Math was just terrible. I used to hate going in in the
   morning and having to face Math. I used to hate it. I hated it.

Or perhaps a few subjects were hated, as was the case with Claire.

Claire: Then when I was in 3A they says, "Right Claire, that is it, we know you're not going to work." Irish, French, and Math—they were the three I hated, so they'd say to me, "Sit down at the back of the class and do what you want, but shut your mouth." For a whole year I did that.

This, however, was the exception rather than the rule. Basically they expressed extreme boredom with an uninteresting curriculum.

Liam: I was bored altogether with it.

or

Michael: It was too slow, just sitting there, just reading. I didn't learn anything from that.

Later:

Michael: Any time you went into that English class, it seemed forever . . . you'd never get out. Too slow.

The young people did not mask their boredom.

Mairead: Right now, he used be so boring you'd fall asleep in the class. One day, right, I was like this [falling asleep]. I did nearly fall asleep, my head just nearly hit the desk. He says, "Mairead, I'm surprised at you." I says "Do you fucking blame me, you fucking put me to sleep every day you come in here." [laughs] He says "What do you mean I'm putting you to sleep?" "'Cause you're sitting there and you're reading a book and we're supposed to listen to you everyday. You know, Commerce!" I says "If you gave us something to do, then we mightn't fall asleep." Half the class, you know, would be like that [sleeping].

It was repeatedly pointed out that boredom with the subject matter is linked to lack of interest, which in turn is linked to nonlearning. The young people point out that it is impossible to learn that in which you are not interested.

Judy: For about half the class you'd be concentrating, but then the stuff would get so boring and you'd be so bored yourself, like you wouldn't be interested in it.

Or, more specifically:

Judy: I liked History. I was interested. I had an interest so I was able to work at it, but most of the subjects I wasn't interested in so I wasn't really bothered learning them, you know.

Lack of interest in the curriculum is readily explained by its lack of relevance to what the young people want.

Paddy: That school! School doesn't learn you. They learn you to read and write and do all that. They don't learn you stuff like that [pointing to a garden trowel he was making].

Even with the passing of time, they are no clearer on what school was all about; in fact, having experienced a taste of what they call the "real life" or "real world," they become more vehement about the absurdity of schooling.

HF: Do you think the things you were taught in school had any relevance to you or was of any worth?
Judy: Not really. I don't think so now. Like then I didn't think so either. I didn't know what we were doing or what the hell we were doing it for, but now I don't think it is any use except for your English and your writing and all that.

The young people's boredom with school and their expression of their lack of interest in the subjects would in itself suggest the lack of a learning process in school. However, they themselves refer to the lack of a teaching process as a constant rather than as an exception. They criticize schooling and teachers directly by arguing that the teachers did not teach. That Claire relates how for a year she sat at the back of the class for Irish, French, and Math, and that Mairead retorts to the teacher "If you gave us something to do, then we mightn't fall asleep" has already been noted. Michael, who was placed in the lowest-grade class in a technical school, describes the class situation.

Michael: If I'd concentrated all the time I wouldn't get any further.

HF: You wouldn't?

Michael: No, 'cause when I was in that class the blokes in there were messers and there were no young ones [girls] in that class, just all boys and ah ... they'd be messing and they'd be talking to the teacher and all that crap. I never made anything out of that. All I got to do was to write down what he wrote down on the board and that was it.

HF: Yes.

Michael: And they were questions—no answers [laughs].

The same situation is presented by the other lads who were placed in the lowest-grade class in a technical school, the dynamics of the group situation giving more vehemence to their criticism.

Cyril: She'd write a load of stuff on the board, "copy that down."

Eamonn: She used to write it in the morning and everybody that came in used to have to write it down.

Dave: Even the Sixth Years [17–18-year-olds].

Cyril: And they wouldn't know what she was talking about.

The "young ones"—that is, the young women—echo the same direct criticism of the teaching process. One young school-leaver who got into constant trouble with the Commerce teacher explains how the trouble started.

Margo: He would never be doing much, he'd never be doing much! He'd just write something on the blackboard and he'd just say, "Do that", and he wouldn't even explain it.

The young people also make a link between having an interest in a subject and liking it, and a teaching and learning process being in action. Progress in a subject is explained by the fact that a pedagogical process was being enacted.

HF: Did you like any of the subjects?

Margo: Irish, Math, and English.

HF: Why did you like these?

Margo: Because you always had to work at them.

HF: You were always able to work at them or you always had to work at them?

Margo: No, you were always doing something—like in the other subjects, you weren't really doing that much.

The early school-leavers' perspective on the curriculum is that it was "boring," "uninteresting," and "irrelevant" and that the teaching and learning process was minimal. It is something that they say they reacted against when in school and that they, in retrospect, can still get angry about.

Dave: I can't read.

HF: You can't read!

Dave: I can't.

HF: So did you learn anything?

Dave: No.

HF: If you wanted to, could you learn?

Dave: I could.

HF: And could the others in the class have learned?

Dave: I can read now, but I can't read that very good.

PERCEPTION OF THE TEACHERS

The overall attitude toward teachers held by the early school-leavers is one of dislike or hatred, while some individual teachers are described as "okay." The perception of teachers is colored by the conflict they have had with them. On closer questioning, a substantial level of complaint is leveled at teachers and at the inadequacy of their teaching skills. The young people link their boredom with the subjects to inadequate teaching.

HF: So when you say you didn't like school, you are really talking about forty minutes of every class, all the work that was there, is it?

Judy: Yes, all the different subjects.

HF: Yes.

Judy: And most of the teachers, like they wouldn't make it interesting. They tell you what to do and you do it—it's not interesting, like.

The lack of a teaching process is blamed directly on the teacher. Some thought that the teacher did indeed have information to pass on but either would not or could not pass it on.

HF: Do you think they have a lot of information to pass on?

Sally: Some of them.

HF: Some of them.

Sally: They have a lot of information, but they don't pass it on right. They should make it interesting so you are able to understand it properly.

or

Paddy: Yes, but the master was calling you up, you know, to look at it [homework]. "How come that isn't done right?"—"I haven't got a clue"—and then he'd show you how to do them and he'd just start muttering "ah ah ah" real fast. I wouldn't understand. I'd be standing there looking at him.

Other criticisms of teachers not teaching were more direct.

Liam: There was one master . . . ah he was a drunkard he was, a wino. He'd come in every morning, and he was like that on the table [head on the table]. We'd be all sitting there and he'd be "Would you shut up. Do your homework."

The young people are insistent in their criticism of the teachers on the basis that they fail to pass on information.

[In group conversation]

HF: We'll fortify ourselves with coffee!

Helen: What does fortify mean?

HF: It just means strengthen ourselves. It just means we'll get a cup of coffee [laughing].

Helen: There now, that's what I mean, isn't it, Gillian? They never explained anything to you. If you asked them a word, they'd make you feel stupid for not knowing it, or tell you you should know. That's what I mean. Now you there, HF, you just explain, they wouldn't; I swear!

The young lads who had been placed in the lowest-grade class and where, according to them, no teaching went on whatsoever are more verbally abusive of teachers.

HF: Why did you hate them [the subjects]?

Cyril: The teacher we had was a stupid bitch.

Eamonn: She used to go asleep in the class.

Cyril: We used to have her dancing around the class with sweets.

Eamonn: If you gave an answer you'd get a few sweets. She used to run around the class like a lunatic, "Sweetie, Sweetie." Then she'd eat the sweets and go back to sleep again.

HF: Was she very weird?

Eamonn: She was a fucking mad one. Not only that, she was a junkie.

To a minority of the young people—in particular to the lads who were placed in the lowest-grade class—the teacher is someone to be broken down, and their success rate was very high.

Cyril: In second year we had a master—a country master—and he had us for two weeks, right. Do you remember?

Eamonn: Ah, yes.

Cyril: And he couldn't cope with us. So then, this big stocky master, came in, right. We were all afraid of him, right. After two weeks we were . . .

[Together]: Wrecking the place we were.

Eamonn: He was a thick.

Cyril: Ah Jesus, we used to be all sitting down the back. Me you and— all sitting down at the back saying "Get up out of that you beardy cunt."

The reactions of the "young ones" are not as violent, but that is not to say they don't look on teachers as people to be broken down too.

Margo: We got the teacher crying once and all, the two of us we did [grinning].

The young people not only refer to their efforts to break down the teachers, but to the teachers' efforts to break them down. On-going psychological battle and psychological torture occurred in the classroom.

Mairead: Like, in school, everyone in the class had cried, bar three of us. They were always at us three to get us to cry. He used always try and make us cry at the board. He couldn't get us to cry. He just roared. You'd be saying "You fucking idiot" [to herself]. You'd feel like killing the fucker, that's all he wants.

For the most part their perception of the teacher is of dislike. When questioned, they criticize them on lack of teaching skills. They argue along the lines of no trade, no respect for no teaching. The young people had least respect for those whom they describe as those who did not engage in a teaching process, who made no effort to teach. Teachers are judged as okay if they took an interest in them individually and wanted them to succeed in school, but these teachers are presented as a minority.

HF: Is it that you didn't have respect for them, or what?

Margo: I would but they never have . . . most of the teachers up in . . . didn't have respect for you. Like they'd say anything to you. "Get out of this bleeding class" and all, you know . . .

HF: So they don't have respect for you?

Margo: No, well one or two of them might, you know, like want you to stay on and all this. The others wouldn't give a shit.

For the young people who are placed in the lowest-grade class and where there is no hope of them progressing at school, no respect is felt for any teachers whatsoever, and so indiscipline reigns and the teacher is the enemy.

Eamonn: The other master couldn't cope with us. Took a nervous breakdown, he did. [laughter]

Cyril: Yes. Ran home crying one day.

HF: So you gave him a nervous breakdown.

MAKING AN EFFORT

The early school-leavers' attempts to achieve marks in different subjects were haphazard at best.

HF: Were you good at any of the subjects?

Margo: Yes, well, I didn't think I was any good until it came to getting the results. Like in Irish I didn't think I was any good. I thought I'd get about 20% or something. When the report came home I got 84%.

HF: That was great.

Margo: Yes, I was delighted myself, I couldn't believe it.

Young people who did attempt to get on well at all the subjects, who passively accepted what was taught, were a minority.

Sally: Yes, I was alright. I did what I was told, but you know, even if I didn't do well, like, I did what I could.

The most striking aspect of the young people's account of the effort they put into progress at subjects was that they felt they had a choice as to whether to make an effort or not. Whether an effort was made or not depended partially on liking the subject.

HF: Were there any subjects you ever got good results at?

Claire: Art, English, and Science. They're the only three I passed in my Group Certificate.

HF: Is that because you liked them, or why was that?

Claire: Yes, I liked the subjects. I liked doing them.

or

Mairead: I was good at English, I was good at all the subjects bar Math. It was on all my reports, "Very good," "Excellent," and all this crack and when it came to Math: "Doesn't work at all. Doesn't try." I wouldn't be bothered. I hated Math.

Making an effort in a particular school subject seemed to be based on whether they thought they could succeed. They felt they had a choice to drop out of a subject and tended to take this option.

Helen: I never done Irish or anything because I couldn't. I didn't even try. I knew I couldn't do it anyway, so I didn't bother trying.

The belief that succeeding in a subject was and always would be outside their ability was only expressed directly by one young person.

HF: And did you like any aspect of school at all? Did you work at getting high marks at it or anything like that?

Michael: Me get a high mark! You must be joking.

HF: There was no possibility of that?

Michael: No.

On further questioning, he blamed the class he was placed in and the poor teaching as the real block to his learning. The others mostly felt that had things been different in school and had they concentrated and had they been interested enough to concentrate, they would have achieved better results.

HF: Would you concentrate on any of the subjects?

John: On Art, I did.

HF: If you had concentrated on them could you have got on okay?

John: Yes.

or

HF: And was it because you wouldn't concentrate or because you weren't interested?

Paddy: I wasn't interested.

HF: And you were interested in Math.

Paddy: Yes.

In summary, the effort to get on well in subjects was haphazard and erratic. These was a general feeling that it was not necessary to make an effort at subjects if you did not automatically like them. If one really disliked a subject, whatever that dislike was based on, it was felt that one could drop that particular subject. Not one young person referred to their intellect as being a problem or a reason why they did not make an effort at school. Lack of interest and lack of concentration were the only personal reasons given for lack of achievement in examinations.

MESSING

When the young people attending school hate it, have little interest in the subjects, and are continually bored and when they claim no teaching process was in progress, the alternative to making a personal effort is to "mess." The messing-type response to schooling has an understood limit to it; it does not extend to "getting into trouble" but remains largely as a creative response to boredom, as a means of tolerating boredom. It is not behavior that is directly oppositional to anything, but an informal response to the formal, the bursting out of the natural exuberance of youth.

For the young women, the type of behavior they describe as messing ranged from smoking cigarettes in class, which is considered adventurous, to dangerous messing such as sniffing gas. Their tales of messing progress in seriousness. Every single person messed in school.

HF: Were there a group of you in the class who used to mess?

Helen: Ah yes, every one of us did. I admit I did have a bit of a laugh [laughing], but I never done anything serious like.

Messing is a group or communal activity, often just exercised to release tension.

Sally: I took the smokes out of his pocket [the teacher] and passed it all down the back of the class, and then when it went around the back they lit it and handed it back up and everybody got a drag!

or

Mairead: The whole lot of us in the class, we'd all get up to the one thing. One day we'd all be quiet, the next day we'd all be mad. We'd robbed his [the teacher's] lunch one time and put it in the bin. He was going around the whole class looking for it. He went mad, he did. You see, the way it was in school, we were all behind each other.

Messing is always having some kind of fun by breaking particular rules, but the intention is not to get "into trouble," though in the excitement this is often forgotten.

Claire: We were sitting in the toilet and we were smoking and we were bunking off class. We were sitting on the cistern so nobody could see our legs under the toilet. We were sitting there and then we started messing. I was trying to get Maria's head down the toilet and she had my arms and someone else had her legs. I flushed the chain, and the screams of the three of us. . . . The teacher came in and she's standing at the door roaring, saying, "Right—out now," and she grabbed hold of me and opened the door and threw me out. With the shock I just looked at the teacher and burst laughing back into her face and she was having murder [i.e. she was extremely mad].

While not wanting to get "into trouble," danger of detection must be present or boredom would not be alleviated, nor would tension be released.

HF: What was the worst thing you ever did?

Claire: We used to take gas.

HF: Take gas?

Claire: From the back of the school.

HF: Out of what did you take the gas?

Claire: Do you know the butane gas, out of the lighters?

HF: Oh, the lighters!

Claire: It's dangerous. I wouldn't go near it now, but we used to take that from behind the old prefabs that were going to get kicked down.

HF: And all three of you would take it, would you?

Claire: It'd really be me. I kept saying, "Come on, we'll try it for a laugh," so we all did it and we took it. You'd just get blown out of your head. You'd get all numb, you'd just be sitting there all spaced out, and I was there messing, picking up a chair, and they were going to demolish the prefabs anyway, so I started putting the chair through all the plastic windows and breaking them all down. The two caretakers, one came that way and one came the other way and they caught me. They didn't rat on me, they left me away [i.e. they didn't report the incident].

or

Liam: See, they have gas in there in the Science labs. You'd put the key in and switch it on. So any time we went to the toilet we'd switch on the gas and we'd be all high on it at the back of the class.

The messing of the young men tends to be more openly conflictual with authority, but without the responsibility for that action having to be taken by individuals. This is possible since messing is a group exploit.

[In a group discussion]

Paddy: And then on all the breaks we were all together. That's when it would all start.

HF: What kind of things would you do?

Paddy: Messing. Running around killing each other and all. We were letting the air out of the master's wheels and got caught.

or

Liam: The master, like, before he'd come in, we'd get all the "Mr. Sheen" [floor polish] and spray it on the floor so he'd slip. He never slipped on it. He always saw "Mr. Sheen" on the floor.

This behavior is operated on the level that it runs a risk of being detected but, yet, it is not desirable to be caught. The more adventurous the deed, the more likely it is to be bragged about, but it is only to be bragged about with friends, and not if caught by the school authorities.

[In a group discussion]

Eamonn: I threw a banger [a Halloween firework that makes a loud sound when it goes off] in a teacher's hood and it blew her hood off and I was nearly caught. He [the Headmaster] searched the whole school for bangers. I threw my bangers away. Mine went down the toilet.

When asked the reason for this messing, the answers are direct and simple.

Liam: Just messing 'cause we were bored, you know.

This boredom is related directly back to the lack of a teaching process, as if there were no possible alternative.

Margo: We were never doing much. So like you'd just be sitting there messing. You'd have to be doing something not to mess.

HF: Why?

Margo: Messing because we were bored, because he'd just write something up on the board and he'd just say do that and he wouldn't even explain it or something.

"BUNKING OFF," "ON THE HOP," AND "TAKING OFF" SCHOOL DAYS

Making no effort at the subjects is not the only response to schooling by these early school-leavers; there are three other alternatives. These young people had their own informal way of removing themselves from what they consider to be an undesirable social situation. Because there are legal and family restrictions on their dropping out of school altogether, they still absent themselves in three ways: (1) they go "on the hop," which means that they absent themselves from school without their parents' knowledge and go "on the streets," which usually means just passing time on the streets; (2) they "bunk off" classes, which means that they absent themselves from classes they particularly dislike by hiding from the teacher within the school grounds or by just not being present in the class in which they are supposed to be. (3) The third response is a gendered one to schooling. The young women refer to "taking off" days, and this occurs even when there are legal restrictions. The young woman does not go to school, because the family needs her to work at home. This happens only with the young women where the mother needs the daughter's help at home and allows the young women to "take off" days. The young women consider this as totally legitimate because there is a real need for them to stay at home and they have the permission their parent(s).

"On the hop," and the rural equivalent, "mitching," both refer to the pupil absenting themselves from school without permission. It can be a group or an individual exercise.

[In a group discussion]
Cyril: I said, "Come on, we'll go into the slots" [gambling casino] and see what the story is. We marched in. We were on the hop.
HF: What?
Cyril: On the hop, right.
HF: What's on the hop?
Eamonn: Mitching.
Cyril: Mitching, right.

All of the early school-leavers had gone "on the hop" at some stage, and a majority went fairly regularly.

[In a group discussion]
Gillian: I mitched for months and months and then I'd go home. I always used to go on the mitch.

or

HF: Did you miss many days mitching?
Paddy: I missed a few years [laughs].

or

HF: The subjects you didn't like—was it just because you weren't good at them?
Paddy: No, I was never in school to cop on what they were about.

Some would venture off on their own, particularly if mitching was not so popular in the school they attended.

Judy: A couple of times I went on the hop.

HF: And what would you do when you went on the hop?
Judy: Just walk around.

Usually those for whom going "on the hop" was a more frequent activity knew where others were or where there was a good chance to find others engaged in the same activity.

Niall: On the mitch.
HF: What would you do? Hang around?
Niall: You'd always know someone.

or

[In a group discussion]
HF: What would you do? Were you just hanging around?
Paddy: Down by the river, or that.

"Down by the river" turned out to be one of the few green areas in the council estates where these young people were from, and every day, particularly in fine weather, small groups of school-going young people were to be seen there "on the hop" from school. Other times these young people, particularly if they had money, would venture into the city center.

[In a group discussion]
Cyril: We went into Funderland [games center]. Lost the whole lot, right.
HF: Fifty pounds!
Cyril: Fifty pounds.
HF: On the poker machines? Did you ever lose that much before?
Cyril: Yes, I did.

Taking "days off" is distinguished from going "on the hop" and was something that the young women talked about.

[In a group discussion]
Helen: I didn't hate it, but I didn't love it, it [school] was alright. I

never used to be in, like. I was never in for the full five days a week, you know. I'd only be in about three.

HF: When you weren't there, what would you be doing?

Helen: I used to find something to do so me Ma wouldn't send me. I'd scrub the floors, make the beds. I'd do anything so as she wouldn't send me.

HF: So she'd know you were missing days?

Helen: What?

HF: Your Ma, she'd know you were missing days?

Helen: I never went on the hop. I never went on the hop once in me life [indignant].

School was something from which they took off as many days as they possibly could.

HF: Did you miss many of these days up until Christmas? Did you get out of going as often as you could?

Mairead: Yes, I only went for about three weeks in all, three or four.

Other times these young women did not have much choice in the matter.

HF: Did you like school?

Ita: No, well, it didn't bother me. I was never in. I was out every Thursday.

HF: Why was it you took a day off Thursday?

Ita: 'Cause me Ma was going into town and she needed somebody to mind the kids for her.

"Bunking off" class usually means hiding in the toilets. It is taken in a lighter spirit and can, once again, be either a group adventure of a "messing" nature or an individual's direct way of avoiding a class.

[In a group discussion]

Gillian: When I used to go in in the mornings, if I didn't want to do a subject, I used to sit on the toilet until it was over.

or

Gemma: Yes, I never really went into their classes. Used to always take
off their classes and go into the toilets.

The detection of absenteeism is surprisingly poor.

HF: How long were you mitching before you were caught?
Niall: Three months.
HF: Would they notice you were gone?
Niall: Yes.

or

Paddy: I done four years [at second-level school] but I was hardly ever
in.

or

Gillian: I done half the first year [at school], half the second year, and
half the third ...

One young woman's reply threw the onus back onto the teachers.

HF: And could you do that, would they notice you were gone.
Gemma: Yes, but they wouldn't care.

GETTING INTO TROUBLE

There is a concrete distinction made between "messing" and getting "into trouble," even though the messing behavior can diverge
to "getting into trouble" quite readily. Getting "into trouble"
means that the young person has been detected by the school
authorities as a "messer" and subjected to some kind of formal
punishment. The punishment used on these young people usually
involved either suspension from school for a few weeks, which
is termed by the young people as being "thrown out," or writing
out pages, sometimes from telephone books or sometimes from

ordinary books, which these young people term as "punishment scales."

Suspension was usually the worst form of punishment for the young people because it usually meant hiding from their parent(s) the fact that they had "gotten into trouble" at school. Letters from the school to the parent(s) were usually torn up to avoid detection.

[In a group discussion]

Margo: He says, "Right, you're suspended." Oh, I was in bits, I said "I'm not going home." I was only after getting kicked out of school. I had a feeling me Ma would say something, or even my Da, you know.

Gemma: I would have liked to have stayed in school. I loved school I did, but some of the teachers I didn't get on with and I couldn't keep my mouth closed and I had to answer them all back, all the time. That's the way I am. I don't know what it was.

Liam: They used always pick on me. You mess one day and they're all on you for the rest of the year.

Others, though, opted for making trouble as their actual response to schooling. They were not trying to get out of trouble. This refers chiefly to those placed in the lowest-grade classes.

[In a group discussion]

HF: So you were always getting into trouble?

Cyril: Ah, it was great.

Eamonn: Yes. It was great.

HF: And was that what you wanted—to get into trouble. Why?

Cyril: Because there was nothing else to do.

A majority of the young people had got "into trouble" fairly regularly. Once isolated as a troublemaker or as a ringleader of troublemakers, it seems to have been impossible for the individual to stay out "of trouble" for long, even if they had the best of intentions.

Gillian: I was in _____ Secondary School, that was the first girls' school I was ever in. I was in there five months and I got suspended three times and thrown out twice. They brought me back once and then threw me out again. Then I went to _____. I was dying to go there. As soon as I went there they threw me out again.

CONFLICT WITH TEACHERS

It was mostly through incidents of open conflict with teachers that the young people got "into trouble" that resulted in their suspension. These incidents range from open confrontation with the teacher arising from disobeying orders or using abusive language to physical violence. Gemma describes one of the many incidents of direct disobedience that served to get her suspended. Having got a bad conduct sheet and knowing that for certain it would mean she would be suspended again, she explains;

Gemma: I was telling my Commerce teacher I was going to rip it up and she kept saying, "You rip it up and you'll see!" and I kept saying, "I'm going to rip it up." So I ripped it up.

Judy gives another example.

Judy: She wanted me to apologize because I wouldn't read right. I wouldn't apologize because I didn't really do anything wrong.

The majority of the young people got suspended at one stage or another for use of abusive language to their teachers.

Joe: If you didn't get everything right they'd start shouting at you.

HF: And would that happen often?

Joe: It was nearly happening every day.

HF: Every day, so did you hate that?

Joe: Yes . . . I'd tell them to shut up and all and start shouting at them.

or

Gemma: They'd start telling me to do this, that, and the other, and they wouldn't explain it so I'd start giving them backchat.

Actual physical attacks on the teachers are also described.

[In a group discussion]

Paddy: We'd be messing 'cause we were bored and the teacher would hit you and you'd hit them back and all.

HF: Hit them back! Did you hit back at teachers?

Paddy: Once I did.

HF: And what happened then?

Paddy: I got thrown out, I did, for two weeks.

HF: But would a teacher not have been much bigger than you. How would you manage to hit them back?

Paddy: Throw a chair at them or something.

"FREAKING THE HEAD" AND "RUNNING AMUCK"

"Freaking the head" and "running amuck" are two terms used to describe physically aggressive oppositional behavior directed against the schooling system. Both types of behavior are severely violent against the schooling system and its representatives. "Freaking the head" basically describes behavior in which the young person loses his or her temper and executes mental or physical violence either on school property or on the teacher. Usually the outburst is in reaction to a feeling that the teacher is mentally "putting them down"; alternatively, it is a reaction to the teacher physically hitting them. Both young men and young women had "freaked the head" on occasion. This behavior usually led to instant expulsion.

[In a group discussion]

Gillian: I freaked the head. I threw paint all over the place and knocked down all the presses in the art room.

HF: Why?

Gillian: To get thrown out, that's why I done it. I'd have done anything to have gotten thrown out of school at that time.

This behavior involves more than a defensive reaction. It is a reaction of open aggression, of a mental and physical battle against the powers that be. The example related by Mairead best encapsulates the motivation for "freaking the head."

Mairead: Like when I walked in the door, right, first day in his class and he says, "Here comes trouble." Like he thought he knew me and I had never even set eyes on the chap before. The first time I ever seen him was when I walked in that door. "That looks like trouble," he says. So I says [to herself], "Right, well, fuck you, if you ask for it you have it." From that day on I gave him some fucking life. I was real quiet but then because of that I just kept freaking the head in class.

HF: So would you consider that you were defending yourself?

Mairead: Like for what he said, I got him back for it. He asked for it, so I gave it to him.

Initially there are probably defensive reasons for her oppositional behavior, but the method she adopts in "standing up" for herself is more aggressive than defensive. She defines "defensive" in aggressive terms in that she believes defending herself against insults actually demands giving back more insults than she received. Winning confrontations becomes important.

There is sometimes a substantial group dimension to "freaking the head." Sometimes there is a feeling of moral right on their side in reacting against a teacher.

Sally: There was a fella in our class and he was handicapped. He used a wheelchair, and we all got on well with him. We all liked him. We didn't treat him different. The master said, "Just because you're handicapped you think you're going to get special treatment." With that we all freaked the head. None of us would work, you know. We ripped up our books and all.

More spectacular is the description given of "running amuck." The origin of the reaction is unclear, but the conflict overflows and snowballs into what is referred to as "running amuck" and is tantamount to rioting violence.

[In a group discussion]

Cyril: Something happened one day and we had the whole school running down all the corridors.

Eamonn: Ah yes, I brought a Shetland horse into the school one day. A little Shetland and I let it go and it was running around the school.

Cyril: No not that day, another day. The whole bleeding school went
    mad. We were all going to bash the masters one by one. All the fifth
    and sixth years [16–18-year-olds] all around shouting and singing,
    "One, two, three, four, what the fucking hell is this?"

These descriptions of violent reactions to schooling are at the
farthest point on the continuum of oppositional behavior enacted
against the schooling system and its representatives by the young
people.

2

Early School-leaving

Leaving school early is the obvious outcome of the schooling experience as described in the previous chapter. The current chapter presents the actual process of early school-leaving as described by the young people. It describes how it came about that they left school early, the decision-making element, the family precedent of early school-leaving, the parents' involvement, and the local influence on the action of early departure from school. Overall, individual reasons for leaving school basically follow a pattern of leaving school to go to work. Whether the departure from school was primarily motivated by the desire to escape schooling or, alternatively, was motivated by the desire to work may have varied from case to case, but each young person argued that they left school to work.

EXPULSION

In some cases it was felt by the young people that no decision was involved in leaving since they had been expelled. The young people placed the responsibility of their expulsion on the institution.

Margo: She [the Head nun] was just always on our backs. See, at that
   time we had to get coats and there were four of us in school and me
   Ma just didn't get the coats at the beginning of the year. She was
   always moaning, so me Ma went up and explained that she couldn't
   get the coats and she just goes, "Ah, well they have to get the coats"
   and me Da then went up and she told him that she didn't want us
   coming back.

When placed in a situation like this, the young people were on the
defensive and progressively got themselves into more trouble.
They tended to retort in a personalized abusive fashion to what
they regarded as the nun "picking" on them for not having bought
their coats. This process or reaction ensured their expulsion.

Margo: [Regarding her twin sister] Yes, she hadn't got her coat, so she
   used to suspend her, so I'd say something to her and she'd suspend
   me as well.
HF: Like what would you say?
Margo: Tell her to shut her mouth or something, call her a spectacly
   cunt or something.

Because of their belief that the Head nun was directly in the wrong,
this was excused by the parents.

Margo: Me Ma didn't mind 'cause she knew what the nun was like.
   She was an old bitch.

"WALKING OUT" OR "GETTING THROWN OUT"

The reason for leaving school seems to be that a conflict situation
just gets out of hand; the young people feel they had been victim-
ized to some extent, perhaps having been isolated as a leader of
"messers," and they react badly. The "walking out" takes place in
the heat of conflict without forethought—an impulsive reaction.

HF: What age were you when you left school?
Gemma: Fifteen.
HF: And why did you leave school at that stage, was it because . . . ?
Gemma: I didn't leave, I got thrown out.

HF: You got thrown out. What happened?

Gemma: I had a big fight with one of the teachers. . . . She [teacher] says, "You have your choice, go into your class or leave this school," so I just walked out of the school.

Those who were expelled resented the fact, but both of these young women above felt they wanted a second chance, and the fact that they felt they had not made the choice to leave made a difference to them. Others who had been thrown out reacted in a different way by proclaiming that they had been thrown out because they wanted to get thrown out. This approach enabled the individual to claim more control over the action.

[In a group discussion]

Gillian: Why did I leave school! I got thrown out of school.

HF: You got thrown out?

Gillian: I'd have done anything to have got thrown out at that time.

Cyril explains that having robbed money from his mother he had gone "on the hop" and spent it; she brought him down to the headmaster where the following incident occurred.

Cyril: He turned around and said to me, "I'm suspending you for the rest of the term and come back for your Group Cert." I marched over to him and said, "Well, thanks very much. I'm delighted. Well fuck you and your school." I was delighted. I was waiting for this day to turn up. I walked out and . . .

Getting "thrown out" of school can have a bravado element to it as expressed by Gillian, but this is only a small minority situation. The young people mostly feel a loss of pride if they are told to leave. On the whole they prefer to walk out before being told to leave.

Gemma: So I was thrown out of school the first time [suspended] but then I had my choice to get thrown out or stay in, but I just left, I walked out.

or

Paddy: Me Da was going to get me back in and I went back in and the same all happened again and this time I says, "You're not throwing me out, because I'm going." I just went.

"IT IS VERY HARD TO EXPLAIN"

Some young people just do not seem to know what happened or why they left school. Their descriptions entail an element of individualized mystery. An actual lack of identifiable cause for their leaving is expressed. Once again, a lack of thought before action is apparent.

Bridie: I remember having the school uniform on me that Monday to go to school and I actually felt that I have to go to school and a note came through the door saying to be down at 10 o'clock to start a course [AnCO (a Government Training Body) workshop]. I just took off my school uniform and went. Now I regret that. I always regret that.

Helen, on the other hand, gives a more personalized account of what was happening in her life at that time, but no account of a decision is given. One of her friends had died in a "joyriding" incident, a practice in which young people steal a car with the intention of being in a car chase when the Gardai [police] attempt to follow the stolen car.

Helen: It's very hard to explain. I went to a funeral and I was real upset. I just never went back to school. I was glad at that time. I just didn't care.

HF: What did you do, did you just stay at home?

Helen: I just stayed at home, yes.

"I'D HAD ENOUGH"

These other young people who left of their own accord describe their leave-taking as being due only to dislike of school. This can be considered as a "push" factor—they left school because they wanted to get away from schooling; their schooling was responsible for their wish to leave. It was dissatisfaction with their schooling situation that was the primary motivation.

HF: And did you get kicked out in the end?

Eamonn: No I left. I'd had enough.

Mairead expressed her dislike of school straight away. She intended to leave as soon as possible. She talks about a conversation held with the Career Guidance teacher.

Mairead: She said to me, "How long are you planning on staying in this school?" "I'm not staying for six months," I said. "I'll leave by two months. As soon as I can I'll leave." ... I got my Christmas holidays and I never went back.

This hatred of school sometimes involves a feeling of "getting nowhere."

[In a group discussion]

HF: In the end why did you leave?

Joe: Because of the Group Cert. I didn't get the yoke, and I didn't like it at school.

HF: So why did you leave in the end?

Judy: I was passing most of the subjects, just passing, you know. So long as I got enough to pass it was all right but, ah, I didn't really get great marks in any of the subjects.

HF: Right, Dave, why did you leave school in the end? You left after one year, was it?

Dave: I did first year and I reckoned I was getting into too much trouble.

HF: With the teachers, all the time?

Dave: Yes. I was getting bad reports and there was a job going down in the dairies and I got a job down there working in the mornings.

"I GOT A JOB"

The second motivation in the school-leaving process, of equal importance as their dislike of school, is their interest in finding employment. None of the young people left school without first looking for employment. For each of these young people, the alternative to school was working, and there was nothing acceptable between the two. They usually left school when they had acquired employment or to acquire employment. In most cases, the young people chose employment above schooling.

HF: So, in the end, did you leave after the Inter Cert [Intermediate Certificate Examination]?

Liam: Yes, I got a job. I got a job there during the summer, last summer, and I did six months . . .

HF: And did you leave school because you got a job?

Liam: No, I got my Summer holidays and it was around August. I go back in September and I got the job in August, so I didn't go back then. I couldn't stand it any more.

As can be seen, very little cognizance is taken of a decision-making process. Once a job is found, the outcome is to some extent inevitable. On further discussion with Liam, an element of choice is still not apparent.

HF: Did you make a choice to leave or . . . ?

Liam: I would have gone back and gone on to do my Leaving, but in a way I was delighted to get out of school.

HF: Why?

Liam: I just was, I couldn't stand it, you know.

Judy's action of leaving school is described in almost exactly the same words as Liam's.

Judy: Then during the summer I went to look for a job. I got a job, so I left. I didn't go back.

Others just waited to reach the legal age at which it is possible to quit school and then they looked for a job.

Claire: I got thrown out loads of times and then, on my fifteenth birthday, I knew that was the legal age I could leave school. I told them I was leaving, I was going looking for a job.

While these young people wanted to leave school because they disliked it, finding a job was taken very seriously even in these early days of school-leaving. Michael expressed that he was not learning anything anyway while staying in school, and proceeded to describe his departure from school.

HF: And then what happened that you eventually left?

Michael: I went to a job, a job discussion before I left, down in the bakery, and your man says, "Come in tomorrow morning."

HF: Yes.

Michael: And my auld fella told me that there was a bus leaving at six o'clock and it would be there by half-six, because I was meant to start at half-six. There was no bus. I had to walk in there. By the time I got in there, it was a quarter to eight. And your man says, "You can go home and sleep it off," and he meant that I didn't get it.

PARENT'S INVOLVEMENT

Since these young people were minors when leaving school, their parent(s) enter into the explanation as to why they had left school early. In the cases where the young person was labeled a "trouble-maker" and expulsion was in the pipeline, the parent(s) were heavily involved in the situation and usually brought about the final parting. This occurs because the school authorities would have contacted the parents if a the young person was to be suspended. The parents would go to the school to defend their son or daughter or to get to the root of the problem. The mother was the one who went to the school in the initial stages. If relations between the mother and the school authorities reached a stalemate, the father played his role (in those cases not involving single parents). In Gemma's case, she had been labeled a "troublemaker," and, while she did make trouble, her objection was that she was the only one receiving punishment. The story continues:

Gemma: Me Ma went in that Wednesday. She was called into the office and she goes. She says, "Its not fair to keep picking on Gemma. She's not the only one. I'm keeping her out of school now."

In the cases that led to expulsion or "walking out," the parents' involvement in negotiations resulted not in a reduction but in a heightening of conflict, as was the case for Gemma. Paddy explains the part his parents played in his leaving school. Paddy had "had enough" of doing punishment work and would not complete the punishment work he had been given to do. He, therefore, got suspended, and the parents then got involved.

Paddy: Yes. See, me Ma and Da never believed me when I used to come home and say, "I got this for nothing" and me Da would say, "You don't get anything for nothing now," you know. My Da went up to the school and had a look at the scales [punishment work] and he went mad, he did. He took my little brother out as well.

HF: How come your Da went up?

Paddy: Me Da started going up after me Ma. Like me Ma used always go up. Me Da never went up, he wasn't bothered with the school. And me Ma then went up to the Headmaster and he started roaring at her, "He's always messing" and all that. My Ma says, "Don't fucking shout at me you bastard" and all that. He says, "Get out, get out of this school and never come back with your sons." My Da goes back up later on.

HF: He said that to your Mother?

Paddy: Yes. My Da went up later on and gave him a black eye, punched him around. It was at the break, the ten-minute break, and all the young ones on the corridor saying, "Go on, go on."

HF: Did he bring any action against your father for hitting him or anything like that?

Paddy: No, he started it.

HF: Yes.

Paddy: He started roaring and all and me Da just got fed up with it.

While negotiations were usually already close to an end before a father entered the arena, his involvement would conclusively and effectively end them.

In a majority of cases the parents seem to have been disappointed in their children's leaving school early, regardless of the conditions under which they left.

HF: Would he be disappointed in you?

Margo: Yes, he goes mad he does. Me Ma does too. She was used to it though. We were always getting suspended from _____, for the least thing, having no shoes or no coat or something.

There is a sense of the mother just giving up the effort:

[In a group discussion]

Margo: Me Ma said she could have got us back in but she wasn't bothered, all her trouble, and we'd be only, you know, messing all the time again.

or

HF: What did your mother say?

Gillian: She'd kill me. Then she'd stop, she gave up with me.

Whether or not parents wanted their children to stay in school made no impact if the young person wanted to leave. There was no way the parents who wanted their children to stay in school could force then.

[In a group discussion]

Helen: My Ma was dead keen on me staying in school. She wanted me to stay in school until I was eighteen. There was no way I wouldn't stay in school until I was eighteen.

or

HF: How come she did not want you to leave until you were fifteen, but didn't mind after fifteen?

Claire: No, she wanted me to stay on and do my Inter Cert and all that. Nobody can force you to stay on in school. I could have been thrown out loads of times and they wouldn't have stuck me [tolerated me].

Even the most valiant attempt of a parent would be fruitless, and the parents would cease trying to stop their children quitting school.

HF: What did she think of the whole thing—was she mad with you?

Gemma: Yes, she was going to keep me in for a month and all. She kept me in for a week and I was going mad, I was. In all day. I wasn't allowed out the door. So then she says, "Well, if it wasn't all your fault, I'll let you out." This was after a week. The teacher had nearly had her in tears, and all over me.

For the most part, the parents just had to accept the situation that school was not what their child wanted.

[In a group discussion]

HF: Did your parents say anything about you leaving or your family?

Sally: Me Ma was giving out.

HF: What kind of giving out?

Sally: Like, you're not leaving.

HF: Did you have to wait until she agreed before you left, or did you just leave?

Sally: I told her I was going to leave anyway, so she told me I could leave then. She knew I hated it. She was against it even though she let me go in the end.

HF: Your family—did they care that you left school, or did they want you to, or was it your own business, or what?

Judy: Me Da wanted me to stay at school. I hadn't any interest in school, like I wasn't going to get anywhere staying in school so me Ma told me Da I was leaving. I had left and that was the end of it you know.

HF: Was he angry?

Judy: Yes he was mad. He didn't say too much, like. Just "You're too young to be leaving school."

For those parents who did not want their children to leave school the situation was alleviated if, and when, the young person got work. The parent(s) considered work a viable alternative to school if the young person was leaving school despite parental opposition.

[In a group discussion]

HF: What did you do then, just stay at home?

Helen: I just stayed at home, yes.

HF: What did your parents say when all this was happening [leaving school]?

Helen: It's only me Ma is there.

HF: What did she say?

Helen: She used to say, "You're going back to school or you better get a job, but you're not staying here all day doing nothing." But I never did go back to school, and I never did get a job either.

or

Dave: She let me leave because I got a job down in the Dairies.

The parents would usually make their children go back to school if they did not get a job.

HF: Were you just at home then [after leaving school]? Did you have to work at home?

Claire: Not really, every day me Ma would say, "Do the hoovering" or "Make the bed," something easy or "Get out and look for a job. If you don't get a job soon you'll be back to school."

HF: So she wasn't too angry with you?

Claire: She brought me back. That's when I left school when I was fifteen. I couldn't get a job. She brought me back and says to the master, "Will you take her back" . . .

Only a small minority of parents approved of their children leaving school. Liam's parents approved on the basis that he was getting into trouble after school while hanging around and that work would keep him out of trouble.

HF: So what did your parents say when you were leaving school? Did they mind?

Liam: No, they were delighted, they were.

HF: Because you'd be making some money?

Liam: Because I'd be making some money, getting out of trouble, you know.

HF: Getting out of trouble?

Liam: Getting out of trouble. Because I was messing, but I haven't got into trouble since I started working.

Ita's parents actually instigated her leaving school early.

HF: You left and did your parents say it was okay?

Ita: Me Ma was the one that put the idea into my head, she made me get a job.

Only two sets of parents were said "not to care" whether their children left school early.

Eamonn: They didn't care much.

or

Joe: They didn't mind really.

However, even when parents were most adamant that their child should stay in school, the young people felt that the parents had not given them good reasons for staying. They felt that there had been little explanation as to why it would have been better for them to stay.

Judy: Me Da would have liked me to stay in school. He wanted me to do me Leaving and all, but none of these explanations why, you know.

If the parents' schooling history was known to their children and it was not one of school-going, the young people could use this information to argue the merits of leaving school early.

Gemma: Like me Da, he never went to school.

HF: So what did he think?

Gemma: He just kept saying, "You should have stayed in school"...
Well, he wants us to go and stay in school, but he can't read or write.

SOCIALIZATION INTO EARLY SCHOOL-LEAVING

These young people through their family and neighborhood had experienced only early school-leaving, so much so that they had their own definition of what it is: leaving before the legal age limit or before completing their Group Certificate Examination.

[In a group discussion]
HF: Did they leave school kind of early too?

Sally: Yes, they did leave early. Only one of my sisters stayed on. She did her Inter.

or

HF: Had they left school early too?
Mairead: No, they had done their Group Cert.

Early school-leaving followed a precedent of early school-leaving on the part of the rest of the family. The older members of the family usually left school early, although there was one notable exception: Gillian had an older brother who went on to third-level education. None of the other young people even knew people who had gone on to third level.

Mairead describes her family's history of early school-leaving, which is typical except for those who are the eldest in the family.

HF: Had they dropped out of school very early, or what?
Mairead: Most of them, nearly everyone of them. Like my brothers were always doing a bunk off school. Never went to school. Me Ma would leave them in and they'd run back out. My sisters all left early. They all got jobs. They're all married now. Tommy he done six months like myself. M____ I think done six months. P____, I think he done three years. He was the only one in the family.

Their definition of early school-leaving comes not only from their family background but from the experience of their friends, the labor market, and their entire neighborhood background.

[In a group discussion]
HF: You know the four of you who were in school together, did they all leave school early?
Joe: Yes.
HF: All left school, and what do they do?
Joe: Two of them is working and one is doing an AnCO course.

or

HF: Did many of your friends leave at the same time as you did?

Sally: No, some of them stayed on and some of them left before me.

The factories in the locality employ young early school-leavers in large numbers.

HF: Did you think you were very young to leave school then?

Judy: No, I didn't really think that at the time because a lot of young ones like that did leave school. Like around the factory—there were loads of factories where I was working and they were all around my age.

These young people are surrounded by a community of early school-leavers. They do not feel that by leaving school early they were in any way unique.

[In a group discussion]

HF: Would you say that [leaving early] happens a lot around here?

Gillian: Nearly everyone is leaving school very early.

Helen: Especially on our road. There's no one in school, kids and all that never went to school. Jesus, I swear to God. Me, I do be saying, "Why aren't you at school," and me like, you know, I'd be laughing at myself [laughing].

AFTER TWO OR THREE WEEKS

Having left school, each young person recalls practically the exact same reaction: immediate exhilaration, followed by complete boredom.

[In a group discussion]

HF: Did you feel free when you left?

Mairead: I felt great [laughs]. It was brilliant. I used to love getting up in the mornings. Me Ma couldn't believe me, hopping up out of bed, you know.

HF: Did you think of what you were going to do?

Mairead: No, I don't think I'd any cop on. I didn't think it was going to be so hard to get a job. . . . You know how it was. When I left school it was great because my mates weren't working but when my mates got a job, I nearly got sick. I was sickened I was.

Those who most hated school felt the greatest relief to have left, but idleness was not what they wanted.

HF: Were you delighted to have finished with school?

Martin: Of course, it was great. I thought it was great at first but after about four or five weeks I really got pissed off, you know.

Even though they had been forewarned, this did not affect their decision.

[In a group discussion]

Helen: Yes, and as soon as I left school I was bored [laughs].

Gillian: My Ma always told me, "You're going to be bored sitting around." So I got a job then a month after, so I wasn't too bad.

Only one person actually missed the challenge of schoolwork, despite how bored they all were on quitting school.

Margo: At the start I felt, ah, Jesus, this is great, no more school, no more getting up in the mornings and facing them. Then after two or three weeks I'd have loved to be back in school.

HF: Why was that?

Margo: Leaving, I didn't miss it for the first while. I was delighted. Then I started missing the bit of crack we used to have in school.

HF: You didn't start missing the schoolwork though?

Margo: Well, in a way I did. Like, I was sitting here doing nothing all day and I missed the maths. The maths and the Irish.

Their boredom for the most part was connected with not having their friends around them or not having been successful regarding finding work. The initial boredom or perhaps disappointment did not tempt any of them to return to school.

3

Work Experience
and Future Prospects

The previous chapter has described the process of early school-leaving. It has been noted in this description that the young people's perspective on work has a direct bearing on the process of their early school-leaving. This chapter embarks on a portrayal of the early school-leavers' attitude to work, their actual labor market position, their individual work experience, and the financial rewards of that work experience. In addition, the family financial situation is explored, since this is obviously relevant to work attitudes, particularly in economically subordinated groups.

PERCEPTION OF WORK

The young people's perception of work is decidedly complex and gendered. Work is definitely a symbol of adulthood for them all. On attaining employment they achieve an independence that is of major importance. In the young men's view, it raises their status.

Liam: I was working with all men and all. You don't get anything out of it, like a trade, but you get a bit of muscle into you, lifting all that stuff.

Work is something that is never spoken of in a trivial manner. There is almost a reverence for manual work among the young men, and some who had not talked freely about their school experience went to great lengths to communicate their interest in it.

HF: Why do you like metalwork so much?

Michael: Why? Because it's hard and yet you can take your time at it. There's no rushing. You can get the whole thing made whenever you want, you know what I mean? You have the whole work class and if you don't get it done today, you'd have to do it tomorrow. When I do metalwork, time flies. So I hope I can get the whole thing done today or else do overtime, but you can't do overtime in here. It's hard work, but it's great hard work.

The young men have an idea of work as being hard, tough, and manual. White-collar work does not come into the sphere of their vision of work. Occasionally they might refer to office work, but only in a derogatory or derisive way.

[In a group discussion]

Paddy: I wouldn't do an office job. No way.

The young women's perception of work differs to a slight degree from that held by the young men. Like the young men, they reject white-collar work, and this forms a large part of their reasoning for leaving school. Their common view of white-collar work is secretarial work, which they reject unanimously. Claire refers to her "placement" in an office.

Claire: They tried to put me in an office. There was no way I'd go into an office. . . . I'm not interested in sitting in an office all day.

Variations from the young men's attitude occur regarding the acceptability of all manual work. A minority of the young women expressed a discriminating attitude. Gillian would not work in a café; it was not acceptable to her.

[In a group discussion]

Gillian: That's the one thing—I'd never work in a café, that's the only thing I wouldn't do.

HF: Why do you say that?

Gillian: I'd just feel like a skivvy or something—you know, cleaning up after other people.

Another difference is that the same love of hard manual work is not to found in the young women's consciousness. They do not identify with the hard manual work in the same personalized manner.

While the young school-leaver's perception of work is that it is a symbol of adulthood, this understanding was most frequently expressed by the young men. The young women felt a necessary financial responsibility to contribute to the home income on a material basis—the necessity to add to the money needed to rear their younger siblings. The belief that the young people would achieve independence through work by the acquisition of money is the primary motivation in finding employment. The ability to contribute to the home income is a necessity for all these young people.

Bridie: You will find it's not the first three in every family that want to do the Inter and Leaving. It's the younger kids. You've an advantage if you are born the third child rather than the first or second, because the first and second always go out and find jobs. They have to.

The notion of work is entirely intertwined with the concept of an independent income. There was no understanding and complete mystification at the fact that I was unpaid while doing this research. Usually the first question asked was, "How much do you get for this?" In the introductory stages, with each group there were problems with this. Three separate incidents occurred where some of the young people would bring up, in discussion, the subject of the researcher's unwaged status.

[In group conversations]

Jenny: You're mad, I wouldn't come to this kip if I wasn't getting paid. Ask the [manager] for a cheque!

The overall approach to not receiving an income is best expressed by Bernadette in relation to student status.

HF: What, then, do you think of the fact that I'm still going to college?

Bernadette: I think you're stupid. You know, what age are you?

HF: Twenty-four.

Bernadette: You should go out and get a job instead of wasting your time in here. You're not getting paid, you know. That's stupid. I'd rather go and get a job, but it's your life.

Pay or money is central to their perception of work, particularly in the young women's case. Work is a means to an end. It is the "take-home" pay that interests them. There was little talk of work satisfaction by the young women. While there is an attraction in adopting an adult role or in leaving school, the wish to acquire employment is predominantly located in the desire for money, for an independent income.

Work has also an added value for the young people, which they refer to: it "keeps them out of trouble." They have a clear perception that in working there is safety, but without work "trouble" cannot be avoided. Work keeps them off the street, no matter how badly paid, and gives a profile of respectability.

HF: Did you come to the Community Training Workshop for money, or for what?

Joe: To get me off the roads. I was going around robbing and that.

HF: Were you in trouble with the Gardai?

Joe: They know me alright, like I'm up on a charge now, I am.

The young women make the same point.

Margo: Let's say you're working eight to four, like that is getting us off the streets for a while, but then, like, after four there is nothing for us to do . . .

WORK EXPERIENCE

Each young person left school with the intention of finding employment. Sometimes there was initial success. It has already been noted that in some cases they found work in order to obtain permission to leave school. For others, a minority, there was no success. For those who found work, the type of employment obtained was often unsuitable. In the case of Liam, his job was so physically demanding that it was more suited to an adult male rather than a fourteen-year-old. Obviously their employment was part of a labor cost-cutting system operated by companies.

Liam: Delivering washing machines, fridges, and all that stuff. See, I was working a seventy-two-hour week for fifty pounds. It wasn't worth it. I just left. The boss was always picking on me, you know, because of my size.

The type of employment the other young men found was, for example, part-time milk delivery or leaflet delivery, and these were the main areas of employment for under-aged men. The majority of young women acquired work more easily than the young men. They found work in either of two places: the local sewing factory or the local fish factory. The sewing factory was the more satisfactory of the two.

HF: Had you to work hard?
Judy: No, work wasn't hard. We used to have, say, a certain number of skirts to sew. You did that number and that was all you had to do for that hour, you know. Then you could go away and have a smoke or a cup of tea and that was easy enough.

Others found the work difficult if they could not sew. Then they were "on the floor" packing, which was considered hard work. The fish factory was second choice; a few of the young women refused to work there, so it was not work at all costs.

[In a group discussion]
HF: When you left school, did you get a job?
Gillian: In the fish factory.
HF: How long did you stay there?
Gillian: I lasted ages and then the terrible smell caught up on me. I couldn't stick it. At eight o'clock in the morning the smell of bleeding fish, yach, and then cutting its guts out. Oh Jesus!

Others took a shorter time to decide they could not work there.

HF: Would you look for work in the fish factory?

Mairead: I worked there for one night. I couldn't stand it. I was looking at all the guts getting shoveled up and all. I pitied the poor people who had to do it.

or

[In an individual discussion.]

HF: Then you got a job in the fish factory eventually. Did you like it?

Sally: No, it wasn't great, cutting fish open and taking the insides out.

Work in the fish factory was on a seasonal basis, and the conditions were terribly exploitative, as described by Sally.

Sally: We mainly got overtime. You'd get overtime from eight o'clock in the morning and you could sometimes work until nine or ten o'clock that night.

HF: Would you have worked those hours often?

Sally: Yes, nearly every night and then work Saturdays and Sundays.

HF: Are you a work maniac?

Sally: They used to ask us to come in. That's what me Ma used to say—"You never have a job and then when you do, you're a work maniac." I used to be coming home at eleven at night. . . .

HF: Was it for the money you'd do these hours?

Sally: No, it wasn't for the sake of the money. Like she [supervisor] used to say, you're working late. She'd ask for a big explanation if I wasn't working late so you had to.

The work initially contracted, such as it was, invariably lasted only a short while. The work that was part-time by nature, such as milk deliveries and leaflet deliveries, entailed very few hours and very little pay. Work such as the fish factory employment and sewing factory employment was full-time, though temporary, and usually came to an abrupt end. The work in the fish factory was seasonal, and the sewing factory laid workers on and off abruptly in response to market trends.

Judy: I was there nearly a year. Then they closed down a certain amount of the factory because the bosses weren't making enough money out of it. You know. Then I was out of work for a while.

or

Sally: I only lasted six months.

HF: What happened?

Sally: There was no more work so they left me off. It just went slack. He let a few others go as well.

There was a minority of cases where work came to an end due to the employee being fired, on the basis of some kind of conflict. Liam describes how his work came to an end.

[In an individual discussion]

Liam: See, I was working seventy-two hours a week for fifty pounds. It wasn't worth it. I just left. The boss was always picking on me, you know, because of my size.

HF: You got fifty pounds for that much work?

Liam: Yes, seventy-two hours, Monday to Saturday. I was working with a man and he was on a hundred and fifty pounds, same work as I was doing.

Paddy's work came to an end due to conflict also. He describes the situation.

Paddy: I used to work in G_____ and the bastard gave us the sack. You know, I come in three days a week. Then he says, "Start coming in all week, will you?" I says, "Is there any extra pay in it?" He says "No." So I stayed coming in three days a week — the usual. I went in, and he says, "I won't be needing you any more." I says "Why not?" He says, "You didn't do what I told you."

For others the reason behind their leaving or being sacked is more obscure.

Claire: I went out and I got a job for a month and I got sacked out there and it wasn't even my fault I got sacked. It was the supervisor on over us. She was having people on for a month and then sacking them. . . . If she [supervisor] didn't like the look of you, you weren't going to be left there, but if she thought you were alright you'd get on great with her; you'd be left there for years, you would.

THE NEED TO WORK

It was described in the first section how early school-leaving is directly linked to the intention of finding employment. This need to work is based on the wish to attain adult status and most importantly to attain an independent income. The most direct, all-pervasive interest among these young people was their concern regarding finding employment. For those who had never worked since leaving school, the desire was strong and more palpable. Their lack of success at finding employment was a severe disappointment.

We have already recorded (p. 41) Michael's story of how he left school to take up a job in a bakery. However, because the bus did not leave on time, or because his father made a mistake in relation to the bus timetable, he failed to arrive on time for work on the first day. He was fired on the spot, the assumption being that he had a hangover from alcohol consumption the night before. Michael was very disappointed with what he saw as a missed opportunity, the loss of a potential job.

HF: And you wanted to work, basically?
Michael: Still do.

The lack of work in the past leads to a strong wish to work.

[In a group discussion]
Susan: I want work, you know. We all sit around for ages, we do. We're all fed up. Sometimes we all start going over. Will you give us something to do, give us something to do. He's [trainer] always busy himself. . . . At the end they send you out to a job, you know, and one out of ten don't get it. They send a group out, one doesn't get the job usually, but the rest do. So I mightn't be that one. I hope not [this refers to a four-week placement].

This anxiety to work is spoken of freely among both the young men and women. The young women refer directly to money as opposed to starting work as a benefit of working.

[In a group discussion]

Gillian: That's all I wanted—to work and get loads of money, that's all I wanted. I'd love a job now.

Helen: I'd do anything for a job now, and that's being honest. How I'd love a job. I'd rather have a job than to be out of work. I'll go nuts just doing nothing.

The experience of having had no work for a long period is expressed clearly as a negative experience.

HF: How long were you between jobs before you got into the fish factory?

Sally: I was about a year between jobs.

HF: What were you doing for the year you were at home?

Sally: I was out looking for a job. I had no money, it was bad. . . . I just wanted to get a job, you know what I mean. I had no money or anything . . .

HF: Why do you work for thirty-seven pounds now when you were making so much money before?

Sally: I'd prefer to be doing something than sitting at home.

Their interest and anxiety in relation to securing employment is best encapsulated in the following incident, in which one of the young people had attained a "placement"[1] for four weeks in the local supermarket working as a trolley pusher.

[From my diary]

Nelly [trainer] said, "I'm just after meeting Cyril going across the road. He's cheering and singing as if he won the world cup. I asked him what he was so happy about. He said he'd got a job. He was throwing his jumper into the air. I hope no-one meets him or they'll lock him up! He's a gas young lad, isn't he?" I was surprised he was so happy at so little. Dympna [trainer] answered, "It may seem little to you but it's not to him. This is his first chance. He was getting worried he wouldn't even get In-Company Training."

MONEY AND WORK, MONEY AND FAMILY

The motivation to work is inextricably linked to earning money. Money is a regular issue for the young people. To obtain work is to get an independent income, and this is of primary importance to the young people. Obtaining money is expressed as a necessity. Gillian, when asked why she worked in the fish factory, having described her disgust at the work, replies that she needed the money.

HF: Tell me why you stayed there so long as you did?

Gillian: 'Cause me Ma needed the money and I needed the money.

The young people felt that they needed money for themselves, and it was felt that money dictates the whole lifestyle.

Judy: I always had enough money for myself, that's what I liked about working, you know, I was never left without money.

HF: Did you think the most important thing about work was the money at the end of the work?

Judy: Yes, having something for yourself.

or

[In an individual discussion]

HF: Do you think the money was important?

Joe: Yes. Very, 'cause you can't do anything if you've no money.

Usually there is a second motivating factor: they see their position as needing money for themselves and their family.

[In a group discussion]

Gillian: They [family] need it or I need it, you know, to do something. I don't like sitting in every night of the week. You need money, you need money, no matter what, for everything.

HF: How much were you earning a week?

Gillian: It all depends really. If I got seventy pounds I'd give me Ma thirty pounds and keep forty pounds myself. It was alright, it was. The hours were bad though, slaving we were, we were like slaves.

Even those who say that they left school to earn money for themselves include the parents' lack of money as an explanation, because the parents wouldn't have money to give their children. The parents would be glad of extra cash themselves.

HF: Were you going out to find work because you could bring some money home or was it just for yourself?

Claire: Myself. You see, I started smoking and all and she [mother] hadn't the money to keep me in cigarettes. She was delighted I was independent and I could buy my own cigarettes. I wouldn't be bumming off her all the time. She said the money was grand and all. She was delighted with the money [the money Claire contributed to the family].

Each young person earned between £20 and £38 weekly, depending on age, at the Community Training Workshop.[2] When asked what they used this money for, all of them answered that they gave at least half of their money to their mothers. Usually this payment to the family finances is presented as a choice made by the young person. They did not actually say they had to give this money at home, just that they gave it because they wanted to.

[In a group discussion]

Kevin: I give me Ma a tenner.

HF: And do you have to give her the money, or do you just give it to her?

Kevin: No, I just give it to her.

or

Judy: I don't have to, but I do.

However, it was made clear by some of the others that there was not much choice involved, that there was a strong expectation or obligation to contribute money to the home.

HF: What do you do with the twenty-one pounds you get paid here? Do you give some of it at home?

Michael: I give half of it to me Ma. There's nobody here that doesn't give money to the home; you have to.

Yet, on the other hand, it seems that some of the parents are reluctant to take the money from their children. In saying that "you have to" give money at home, this refers to family obligation rather than direct parental control.

Claire: If I came out [of the fish factory] with one hundred pounds a week, I'd say, "There, Ma, there's fifty," but she wouldn't take it. She'd only take thirty-five off me, or if I made sixty she'd only take twenty off me. She wouldn't take half of it. Sometimes she would say, "Give us a loan of twenty pounds to pay the ESB [electricity] bill" or something and I'd give it to her, and I wouldn't be expecting it back; but she'd give it back.

No resentment is felt by the young person, and the mother shows appreciation.

HF: How much do you give your mother now?

Judy: Sometimes between ten to fifteen pounds per week.

HF: But you're only getting twenty-five pounds.

Judy: Yes, I know. I do that and my Ma makes sure I have a couple of smokes, like anytime I'm at home if I haven't got a smoke she always gives me a smoke and stuff like that. She knows I haven't got much for myself.

The money is given because the family need it. A common feature of payday at the Community Training Workshop was that the young person left the Workshop to walk directly over to the local supermarket where the mother would be waiting for money to shop for groceries. This was something the young people did not really talk about, but yet it was clearly visible. The money is accepted out of need in every case, though the young person would not make this explicit until directly questioned.

Claire: I used to give her thirty pounds and it worked out at about forty or fifty pounds for myself. That was alright.

HF: Do you think that was an awful lot to be giving at home?

Claire: I think it's a lot, but, like, I've a good few in the family. Like I've five young brothers and sisters and my Da is out of work, so like I don't mind, you know.

or

HF: Does she need money or are you just paying for yourself?

Mairead: Ah no, she needs it. Me Ma and Da are separated. She doesn't have much money. She's only on the pension.

or

HF: How much money has she coming in weekly?

Claire: Ma, she's not working, and me Da's on Assistance. It was grand when I was working 'cause I was earning loads of money and she really needed it. Now my sister is getting left off [made redundant] and I give her ten pounds out of me wages here, sort of thing, and me brother gives twenty pounds out of sixty.

The young people do not look on half their wages as being a lot for the most part, but talk of when they have to give more than half.

HF: Fifteen pounds, that's half the money you earn. Do you think that's a lot to give at home?

Sally: No, when I was on the labor getting less I gave her fifteen pounds as well.

When the young people could not get work and are not on a wage, or when the wage is as low as given by the Community Training Workshop, the situation usually gets fairly difficult at home. Yet the young people will never say this in a group discussion or without being queried.

HF: So the money is fairly scarce at home these days!

Stephanie: Yes.

HF: Is that bad, or does it affect you?

Stephanie: Yes, it's terrible. If they have no smokes, they take it out on you.

Having given half of their money at home, the young people have about ten pounds left. This they usually spend on cigarettes or occasionally they go drinking on Saturdays. The "going out with friends" drinking is limited financially to an excursion down "to the river" where they drink "two litres," which refers to cheap cider that can be bought in supermarkets as opposed to off-licence [liquor store] premises. Some try to save their money weekly by giving it to their parents.

Michael: I save it. I'll be working here six months, right, so I give it to me Da. Say all that adds up to two hundred and sixty pounds for six months. I give a lend of it to me Da, so that I can get it back all at once. I can't save so I just give part to me Ma and part to me Da.

HF: What are you saving for?

Michael: A motorbike to fix up and sell. It's as well to find something I can do over time.

ALTERNATIVES FOR THE FUTURE

Work experience or lack of work experience limits the early school-leavers' aspirations for their future. Perspectives differ on their future. Some are hopeful and hold what is the most positive response recorded, in that they say they will try in the short term to find work. They were willing to go out and try again to attain employment. There was hope, which at least extended to the short-term future (as with Paddy) due to a faith in the practical skills taught in the Community Training Workshop rather than any knowledge of the labor market position.

Paddy: Like it's a new start, it is, when you come in here. You know it's not like school at all. It's something different.

or

Bernadette: You learn more out of this 'cause you're going to be looking for a job, so you come out of it with something. When I finish here I'll know something. I'll know what to do then and I'll go out and get the job, you know, because I'll know all about it.

or

Joe: I might get a job out of the bakery. Your man said I had a good chance of getting a job in the bakery where I'm doing my placement.

Those who have been laid off from the sewing factory say there will be vacancies again, and they can once again take up sewing.

Judy, on the other hand, who has been doing some basic photography in the Community Training Workshop, says her future hope is to do photography. Others have reached a realization of their social position and life chances. Take Michael, a fifteen-year-old, experiencing what he sees as his present position and his prospects for the future.

HF: What do you think you'll do after the Community Training Workshop?

Michael: Well, when I come out of here, I'll look for a job, but if I can't get one after three weeks looking, I'll go into Jervis Street AnCO to the workshop in there.

HF: What do you think you'll end up doing eventually?

Michael: Well, when I'm sixteen I'll probably go for the Army. My brother's in the Army. He's doing alright. He has a house, he's engaged, he's doing well for himself.

HF: Is it very tough in the Army?

Michael: Yes , they're meant to be. There was a bloke, W.G., he went for the Army and he only stuck two weeks in there. It was twenty-five pounds to get out, but say you were to stay in there for the six months basic training, you'd have to pay up fifteen hundred pounds to get out.

HF: You'd want to be sure that's what you wanted.

Michael: Well, I want to.

HF: You definitely do?

Michael: Yes.

HF: Why, what's good about it? It's quite rough, isn't it?

Michael: I'd say they are, but it wouldn't bother me. I'd stay in it. I wouldn't care at all if they blew my legs off. I'd still stay in it. I wouldn't leave, because that's the thing. That there is the only job you can get around here if you haven't got skills. See, in the Army you need less skills, while in any other job you need more skills. If you haven't got anything else you might as well go to the Army.

Recognizing his social position and its lack of opportunity, he sees the army as being his last chance to start a career. He realizes that his endurance must be his individual strength, and his motivation is the lack of alternative options.

Others have private aspirations regarding careers, but even in expressing this there is a definite awareness of the difficulty there will be in achieving them. The short-term future is not linked to long-term aspirations because initially they need to find immediate employment—any employment. Margo explains that when she finishes her course in the Community Training Workshop she will go around and "look in a few places," but this is unlinked to her future aspirations.

Margo: I'd love to run my own kennels, well I hope I'll try anyway.

There is a tendency also for the young people to have aspirations for future careers but yet to know that they just will not be successful.

[In a group discussion]
Bernadette: I'd love to work with horses. . . .
HF: Do you think you will get work with horses?
Bernadette: Not really, no. I'll have to find out when the time comes.

Thus it is almost as if they have "dreams" that they believe will not come true, but they do not want to have to think about that aspect of the future. Dave straight-forwardly states what he wants to work at and then directly states that he has no chance of finding this work.

[In a group discussion]
Dave: A courier, I'd love to be a courier.
HF: And would you have any chance of doing that?
Dave: No.

THE "DOLE" AND EMIGRATION

Unemployment assistance or emigration are seen as two future alternatives for those who believe there is no employment to be found. The young men who have tried consistently to find work but failed feel, from their own experience, that they have no work future.

[In a group discussion]

HF: Do you think you'll get a job after this?

Kevin: No, I won't. There are no jobs. Not one job; I don't think so, at any rate.

If they cannot find employment, they are aware that they can collect unemployment assistance, which they know they will be entitled to at seventeen years of age.

[In a group discussion]

Cyril: Yes, you won't get a job anywhere these days. It doesn't matter what you did, you won't get a job these days.

HF: Yes, you're going to be seventeen. Will you go on the "labor" straight away?

Cyril: Yes, come December, I'm on the labor.

The fact that they believe there are no jobs affects the young people deeply. In group discussions in particular (as above), the atmosphere is fairly charged with a mixture of anger and depression.

HF: Realistically, what would you see yourself doing when you're nineteen? Would you say you'll have a job?

Stephanie: No.

HF: How would you feel about that?

Stephanie: It really puts you off.

Being of age to be entitled to social assistance payments is looked forward to because it means an increase in income. It seems the main possibility to those who believe that getting a job is beyond their power.

[In a group discussion]

HF: Would you like to be back home every day?

Mairead: I'd hate it.

Helen: I can see myself, right, being on the labor.

Gillian: I'd say the same.

Helen: I'd rather not be, I'd rather have a job, you know what I mean, but that's the way it seems, because I don't think I'm going to get a job.

HF: What about you, Gillian, why do you think you'll be on the labor?

Gillian: Because I haven't enough qualifications, there's not enough jobs, and I'm not looking either, so it's the three. You know what I mean.

The other alternative for those who believe there is no employment is emigration.

Joe: There's no fucking work here.

HF: So what do you see yourself doing in the future? Do you think you'll get a job?

Joe: No.

HF: No matter how hard you try?

Joe: I don't mind 'cause when I'm eighteen, I'm getting out of this country anyway. It's stupid, it is.

Gemma is emigrating at the age of fifteen, as soon as the Community Training Workshop courses end for her.

Gemma: If we find anything we'll stay over there. Like there's nothing in Ireland for anyone. Like in town [Dublin city centre] I have tried everywhere and there are no vacancies.

or

Liam: I'm emigrating when I get to eighteen. There's nothing here for anyone. Me Ma's got a sister in Canada . . .

NO FUTURE

The other alternative is not to consider the long-term future at all. The young people generally evade discussion on the long-term future by simply saying, "I don't know" or "I haven't a clue." When asked questions regarding his future, Paddy deftly avoids answering, or else he deftly avoids his own thoughts on the future.

[In a group discussion]

HF: When you leave here, what pay would you say you'll get?

Paddy: I'd say around forty pounds a week.

HF: And when you are about eighteen, what pay would you say you'll get?

Paddy: I don't know, I could be dead.

Claire expresses this unwillingness to think of the future, not just as a block to questions, but as a way of life.

HF: So, long-term, in the future, if I asked you what you would like to be, would you have any answer?

Claire: No I wouldn't. I haven't thought about it. I just go to one job and then another job. I never think about my future. As it comes, take it.

REGRETS

Two young women had genuine regrets about leaving school. These were the two who had been "thrown out" of school. In retrospect, they felt they had missed out on something important.

Margo: I'd like to go back.

HF: Why?

Margo: To get something out of it, because for what I'd like to do [become a vet], you'd need a lot of school for. Yes, you'd probably need to go to college.

Margo and Gemma both recognize the link between school examinations and finding work.

Margo: Yes, you have to have your Group, Inter, or Leaving going out to find a job. I've none of those, so it will probably be hard to find a job.

or

Gemma: When I go for a job they'll be asking why did you leave school and you can't get a job unless you've Group Cert or Inter Cert and like that's turning you off it altogether saying I should have stayed in school and done that because I'm not going to get a proper job out of it, if I haven't got them.

It is through this experience of looking for jobs and being unsuccessful because employers ask for examination results that the young people came to see the relationship between school examinations and employment.

Sally: I don't know. I'd like to go back, now but it's too late to go back.
HF: Why?
Sally: Back to do the Group [Certificate].
HF: Do employers ask you for that?
Sally: Yes, some people ask you if you have done any exams.

The young women for the most part regret having no qualifications, but only Gemma and Margo regret leaving school. The rest would like to have the qualifications but would not return to school at any cost.

Helen: That was the only thing I was ever going mad about was because I didn't do me Inter. Even then I said I did not care, but I did care. I really did. I mean if someone came up to me now and said, "Do you want to do your Inter [Certificate]," I'd say, "Yes," and I'd sit in all the time and I'd do it. But I wouldn't do it in the class. I'd rather be on me own and do it.

The vast majority of these young people did not have regrets that they had successfully left school, but some regretted the amount of "messing" they did.

Bernadette: When I look back on it, I ask myself, "Why did I fucking mess all the time, and do no study."
HF: Well, would you go back to school?
Bernadette: No, never.

None of the young men had regrets about leaving school. They did not see the value of school from a self-achievement perspective or from a work perspective. Despite the evidence given to them for their unsuccessful search for work, they reject the link between school qualifications and labor market position, either on the basis that there is no work for anyone anyway, or on the basis that there is no link between the school curriculum and manual labor (which is the only labor they are interested in).

[In a group discussion]

HF: Did you think you'd be able to get a job when you left school?

Kevin: Yes, you won't get a job anyway now, these days. School is a load of bollocks. I know a young one with the Leaving Cert and she works in McDonalds, and I know a fella who had nothing and he has a great job, he has. An electrician he is.

Basically, the majority could not wait to leave school, and, for all but two, to return to school would be unthinkable, no matter what the outcome.

HF: If you went back to school and did your Leaving Certificate you would probably get better pay, different jobs.

Liam: I suppose so, but I wouldn't go through it 'cause I'm only wasting my life away going to school and messing, you know, so I'll just learn as it comes along. . . . I'm glad I'm out of school; I mean, I'd never go back for nothing. For anyone in the world, I wouldn't go back to school.

HF: Why?

Liam: Ah, it's just they can't explain anything to you when you're in school these days. They freak the head and go mad.

DECONSTRUCTING
THE AUTHORIAL EMPHASIS

In talking with these young people I found that information was incredibly forthcoming. It was not difficult to have these conversations whether held between two of us or five of us. I come from a fairly similar background, similar enough to not block off communication, but different enough to make it necessary for me to talk to them in order to gain some sense of where they were at and why they were there. The sense of just finding out about other people's lives seemed to be a very positive moment, both for me and for them. They were certainly interested in what I was doing and why, though for multiple reasons I would have been more concentrated on listening to them than they were on listening to me. Was it a positive moment, though, and if so why and how so? They gave me an account of their social circumstances as they saw them, and then I wrote them up as part of this text. It is necessary to look closer at this form of interaction—for example, what about power relations involved in the interaction? What was their motivation in talking to me?

The above conversations were produced by me in relation to others and by others in relation to me. I was the primary agent in this process; while I did not totally direct the conversations, I directed them more often than did any of the other people I have quoted in the above dialogue. It could be said that I played a central role in the production of a moment of self-reflection, of historicizing the decisions these young people had made in their lives—by asking them to reflect on their current conditions and then, in writing up the account, I described and organized what they had said under different headings. Therefore, it is important to record the above as a process of textual production. It should be read not as a straightforward rendering of the reality of others, nor as a simple construction of a sociological report on these people's experiences. I suggest this because recent critiques[3] have convincingly shown that disciplines such as sociology and anthropology, in conceiving of ethnography as representation, have led to the production of the other as object, and the unjustified seizing of the authority of authenticity.

At this stage I would like to recognize the somewhat authorial tone that I have not managed to escape in the commentary accompanying the dialogue. To this end a brief autobiographical note would seem appropriate at this point to rupture any false notion of authority or objective reporting on a "social condition" of the "other." Since knowledge necessarily involves self–other relations, I need to acknowledge that accumulating this knowledge was partly directed by my own desires and fears.

Education was and is a dominant feature of my past, present, and future. In the past it was about my father's desires for our family and the projection of his own ambitions onto us. He himself was involved in nationalist politics, self-educated, often frustrated when he could not articulate as well as others; he felt the need for formal education for the rural population. Was there a desire there for selfish power, and did that have to emerge as competition against the neighbors? Was this the part I was ashamed of? I was determined to belong rather than compete. I remember my own painstaking strategies to be on the side of the other students in the classroom so that I could be their friend, and yet I always made sure that I was not fully like them because I would always get the grades. It is important for me to reflect on this in case these desires are still at play in this project. Do I feel I left friends behind? Is this a personal guilt-trip, an attempt to go back to belong fully or to make it possible in my fantasies that no community lines of loyalty were broken? If this is the psychoanalytical dimension, does it take from or add to the discursive project that I am trying to further?

As important as my relationship of desire is my relationship of fear—my fear at my/their having such a small income, at having so few options for a future. Knowledge of how tough life is on the dole [Welfare] would be a constant from my social perspective. I was always going to be moving on from that. I fear that where some of these people are heading is going to be temporarily/always worse. I don't believe that I/anyone should have to live without hope for my/their future, without plans for a future, or without a decent income, and I do/will live, work, teach, vote towards this end. I have a deep fear of living anything else.

In terms of self-representation, this autobiographical vignette is not seeking to establish authenticity or to create an authorial voice; rather, it seeks to place me within the knowledge process and in the writing of this book. It is not my intention to produce a closure on the question of early school-leavers. Such an intention would be about formulating mastery and rejecting issues of reflexivity.[4] However, I must acknowledge the desire to formulate solutions, to achieve resolution. From a Hegelian perspective, we could argue that this orientation is an integral part of the construction of the knowledge processes. Since knowledge is dialectical, a knowledge process of negation and supersession is involved, so ultimately mastery is a chimera, but the desire for mastery is always (re)present. It is my contention that this inevitable desire for mastery should be harnessed to the desire for social change. This book will, therefore, be constituted as a text that does not seek closure

but invites further writing, further involvement, and further inter-
subjective knowledge. This is one of the reasons why in Part III the
resolutions that I propose involve a politics of "cultural pedagogy"
in which the cultural worker is an integral part of the knowledge
processes involved, given their practical pedagogic role.

A MATERIAL CRISIS?

This text should provide the reader with images of the
subjectivities and identities of these young people, and with a
sense of the predetermined/fixed or open fluid nature of the productive process leading to early school-leaving. The young people
present themselves as serious actors/people—emotional, rational,
irrational, angry, sometimes violent, sometimes silent. Is the process of early school-leaving fixed in both senses of the word? Is
the process fluid, or does it appear open to intervention? Are these
young people cemented into their identities, or are their identities
mobile? Are they satisfied with their everyday lives as they describe them? Can they reflect on their actions? Can they critically
analyze their experiences? If they don't now, would they find it
possible under any circumstances? Do they long for change, or are
they happy with their social lot?

The text can be read not only to glean views of identities-in-
culture, but also to suggest some concrete characteristics of the
material crisis encountered by early school-leavers. These dialogues tell us that pay is experienced as a crucial and primary need
of young people. Work that would keep them "off the streets" and
"out of trouble" with the law (coming from highly policed geographical locations, this is a serious consideration) is the most
difficult thing to secure. The young people who reported that they
had secured temporary work found this work in fish factories,
sewing factories, milk deliveries, and in contexts with similar low-
skill requirements. All had experienced countless refusals of employment, resulting in an unfulfilled desire for work, finance, and
status in their homes and community. The jobs they held were
terminated when business went slack. They describe leisure time
as being restricted to cheap outdoor drinking with friends within
their own neighborhoods. Hopes for the young people lie in being
old enough to receive an income from the state in terms of social

welfare or else in the vague possibility of emigrating. I believe that
the worst form of subordination is expressed when they argue that
they simply cannot afford to imagine a future. These dialogues
record descriptions of recalled events, of episodes in the young
people's lives, and my interpretation of them. They also set the
scene wherein I can identify early school-leaving as establishing
relations of subordination, in that these early school-leavers
present themselves as clearly experiencing economic and social
status subordination.

NOTES

1. Placement refers to government-sponsored training. The person is
"placed" in a company or factory to receive in-service training, and the
government pays her or him a small sum of money.

2. Community Training Workshops are government-sponsored training
units, set up to attract "youth-at-risk," in particular early school-leavers
without any qualifications. It was at one of these workshops that I was
introduced to and held the above conversations with these young people.

3. For an anthropological critique see J. Clifford, "On Ethnographic
Authority," *Representations*, *1* (No. 2, 1983), 69–73. See also J. Clifford
"Introduction: Partial Truths," in J. Clifford & G. Marcus, *Writing Culture:
The Politics and Poetics of Ethnography* (Berkeley, Los Angeles, and Lon-
don: University of California Press, 1986). For a feminist deconstructionist
argument see A. Game, *Undoing the Social* (Milton Keynes, U.K.: Open
University Press, 1991), in particular pp. 27–32.

4. For further critique of the desire for mastery and knowledge as dialectical, see A. Game's critique of sociological fiction in her book, *Undoing the
Social* (1991).

PART II

THE TIES THAT BIND

If we read the previous set of conversations as indicating that school-leavers live out their everyday lives in states of subordination, then we can move on to identifying a political issue here. If one loosely defines politics as the struggle over public and private space, the political aspect is that early school-leavers live in, and struggle over, their interlinked material and discursive locations of subordination. How do I define material and discursive locations of subordination? By a material position of subordination, I refer to "that in which an agent is subjected to the decisions of another" (Laclau & Mouffe, 1985, p. 153). Early school-leaving establishes relations that insert the early school-leaver into a location of material subordination, as argued in the previous chapters. I do not in any way mean to suggest that early school-leaving marks the "origins" of relations of subordination—this work is not concerned with the essentialist search for origins—rather, the focus is on early school-leaving as one social condition or action through which specific relations of subordination are established.

This section of the book addresses the discursive dimension of early school-leavers' subordination. I argue here that early school-leavers occupy a subordinate discursive space. I refer to the argument that an ensemble of discourses—private, public, and academic—have historically fixed early school-leavers in a subordinate position and thus have played a part in establishing material relations of subordination. For example, insofar as current educational discourses actually explain and construct relations of subordination as unavoidable social realities, they stabilize an understanding of these relations as being "just" relations of acceptable social diversity. To be more specific, the act of early school-leaving establishes relations of subordination that are experienced by early school-leavers in their everyday lives as they describe them, but at issue here is the theme that current discourses in education tend either to construct these as acceptable relations of diversity or else fail to construct them as relations of oppression. In other words, they construct "ties that bind" the early school-leavers into their current location.

Part II addresses previous theoretical and academic approaches to early school-leaving. It introduces four approaches taken in relation to educational underachievement and argues, with Fredric Jameson, for "the primacy of the political interpretation" (Jameson, 1981, p. 18). It carries out a reproduction/resistance reading of the conversations of the previous section, in order to acknowledge the historicity, and the social and political import, of the categories and concepts associated with these frameworks. It seeks to move the debate beyond reproduction/resistance theory and the social research approach toward creating a new political project for early school-leavers.

4

Politicizing Theoretical Narratives

The previous chapters should leave the reader with a sense of the cultural and material space in which a particular group of early school-leavers live. The reader should actually be able to sense the productive process of the construction of early school-leavers in subordinate social positions. I wish to proceed in this chapter by taking up the argument that these early school-leavers also occupy a discursive location of subordination. In particular I wish to address academic discourses. Therefore, this chapter focuses on historicizing academic interpretations of early school-leavers and early school-leaving, showing how these mainstream academic discourses discursively construct early school-leavers in subordinated positions.

Here I introduce four academic narratives on educational underachievement in order to analyze the political components of each. The purpose of my historicizing the academic discursive formations on early school-leaving is to glean them for their relevance to a political practice.

A GENETICS DISCOURSE

First there was/is the genetic explanation of why there are early
school-leavers and why they should be placed in subordinate positions. The genetic explanation of educational underachievement
basically evolved from arguments that individuals are genetically
endowed with a biological property of "intelligence." It is the
individual's "intelligence" that ensures success or failure within
the schooling system. Within the psychometric understanding,
measurement and assessment of human intelligence is possible
through scientifically reliable testing. This perspective also entails
an understanding that genetic intelligence is both innate and inherited.

The debate surrounding this theory has become known as the
"IQ debate," that is, the intelligence quotient debate. Intelligence
quotient refers to the name of the test through which intelligence
was supposed to be measured. The history of the debate can be
traced back to the work of Francis Galton in the mid-nineteenth
century (see Galton, 1869). Galton researched the male lineage of
approximately four hundred Victorians of the gentry class and
reached the conclusion that genius was inherited. Galton, and his
pupil Karl Pearson, went on to develop the subject of eugenics, a
subject that sought to discover statistical techniques for measuring
biological and social differences in order to improve the breed of
the human stock. Alfred Binet, in France, produced a work on the
quantification of "intelligence," directing the area away from its
previous purely qualitative terminology. The intelligence quotient
test was devised. There emerged from the French beginning two
distinct strands of mental test, one British and one American. The
British strand is associated with Cyril Burt and extends through to
the work of P. E. Vernon and H. J. Eysenck and is preoccupied
with the relationship between class background, IQ, and the
mechanisms of educational selection. The American strand has
tended more toward questions of race and stratification.

Arguing that there is a qualitative and quantifiable matter called
intelligence, and that success or failure at school is the result of a
person having a high or a low IQ, has been part of an "objective"
and "scientific" justification for relations of subordination. It is an

argument that has been refuted theoretically in academia but still reappears regularly in rightist discourses.

Helen Rose and Stephen Rose (1979) argue vehemently against what they consider the IQ myth. They present a fourfold criticism of this theory. First, they ask whether "intelligence" is a biological property that IQ tests measure. They argue that it is not, that this amounts to the abstraction or reification of an aspect of human behavior and that logical, numerical skills and conformity are all part of "intelligence." While there may be a biology of intelligence, these writers do not see it as a fixed aspect, and the word "intelligence" is not perceived as a biological construct directly related to a genetically ascribed part of the brain. It is said to relate only to a social construct. Second, they argue that individuals cannot be numerically ranked on an intelligence scale. This would amount to a false imposition on an aspect of social interaction. No attempt, they argue, should be made to analyze "intelligence" in linear, ordinal terms. Third, an IQ score cannot be partitioned into a genetic and environmental component; this kind of excuse, and the meaningless mathematization that goes with it, could only be construed as an attempt to reinforce a particular hereditarian prejudice. Finally, research has shown that IQ tests are culturally biased. In summary, they conclude that the entire exercise of applying mathematical techniques to fallacious biologistic theories is problematic and logically unsound.

The genetic explanation of school "failure" would hold that some individuals do not have the "intelligence" to succeed. It leads to the conclusion that lack of intelligence is the reason for nonparticipation in the educational system. If there is no biological proof of the concept of intelligence and, secondly, if there is no statistical proof that achievement at school examinations correlates with the illusory social construct of "intelligence", then this genetic explanation of school failure can be considered fallacious. If "intelligence" as a construct did exist, and if it could then be empirically measured, a further criticism would be that the genetic theory draws a correlation between "intelligence" and social position which is not substantiated by social research. Does the bulk of social research support a genetic explanation of school "failure"?

The Crowther report of 1959 gives evidence of the absurdity of the proposition that "intelligence" and social position correlate. It shows how the majority of sons of manual workers, despite scoring highly in IQ tests and showing high ability, left school at age 16 or earlier (cited in Holman, 1978, pp. 125–126). Another report in Britain, the Robbins Report, conveyed how in a survey of children from working-class backgrounds with IQs over 130, 72% of the sample did not reach third-level education (Holman, 1978). The majority of children from low-income homes do not go to college, even though their IQs are sufficient. The Irish situation further reflects this reality of working-class nonparticipation in third-level education in that the middle classes make up the majority of third-level students and only about 2% of third-level students are from lower-working-class backgrounds.

In short, social research points to the conclusion that the genetic explanation of school "failure" is not a credible or sufficient explanation for educational underachievement among teenagers. "Intelligence" itself is not a biological construct that can be measured, but an abstract social definition of particular traits. Secondly, there is no correlation between what is educationally considered "intelligence" and social position. Finally, educational underachievement is class-, race-, and gender-relative, so to attempt to explain this social phenomenon in individual terms is about taking up a reactionary political position.

The genetic explanation of educational achievement is one that has most decisively supported the discursive construction of early school-leavers in relations of subordination. Pathological explanations involving individual deficiencies have been used traditionally to explain many forms of deviance, ranging from poverty to crime. Explanations involving individual pathological deficiencies, particularly genetic deficiencies, were and are extremely influential. A genetic explanation of educational underachievement is probably the most prevalent within the ethos of education. It gives a static and simple discursive explanation and justification of why early school-leavers drop out of school and why they should be placed in subordinate positions. It discursively constructs early school-leaving and educational underachievement as a "natural" and unmovable fact, rather than as something that is being constantly socially constructed. Insofar as this discourse is accepted, it serves to place the conditions of early school-leavers outside the realm of either transformation or politics.

THE DISCOURSE OF CULTURAL DEPRIVATION

A second, academic explanation of educational underachievement is that of cultural deprivation theory. The cultural deprivation theory of educational underachievement is derived from the cultural theory of poverty. Within a cultural deprivation theory of poverty, poor people are seen to be part of the larger culture but, yet, not sufficiently socialized into that culture. Their insufficient socialization displays itself through the fact that they do not "progress" within that culture. They are deprived of the part of the culture that enables success. The deprived culture is passed on in a cyclical fashion through the socialization of the children, which includes in particular "inadequate" child-rearing practices. The parents, because they themselves are deprived of the cultural "know-how," cannot pass on a technique for achievement to their children; because of this, the children grow into adults who cannot fit into the larger society with all its opportunities for education and advancement.

As the cultural deprivation theory of educational underachievement developed under the influence of educational sociology, it became slightly more complex. A class perspective was introduced to supplement the "bad-parenting" approach. It was now postulated that the operating socialization in a working-class or minority culture created attitudes and values that differed from those of the mainstream culture. The school was seen to function within a middle-class ethos. It would be more favorable to those socialized in a middle-class environment, and, within this framework, working-class kids were seen to be less educable and more likely to fail.

The cultural-deprivation explanation of educational underachievement, or educational "failure" in the contemporary terminology, evolved from the efforts of Western governments to deal with a renewed awareness of poverty in the 1960s and 1970s. This liberal movement was typified in America by a "war on poverty," as declared by President Johnson. Propelled by race riots, the so-called war lasted approximately four years, from 1965 to 1969. Its

financial backing was then severely cut, as the war in Vietnam
gained momentum. In Britain, the liberal swing is best typified in
the 1972 speeches of the Secretary of State for Social Welfare, Sir
Keith Joseph. Expressing himself in deprivation terminology, he
drew attention to the fact that deprivation persists despite an im-
provement in living standards introduced with welfare payments.
In the United States the problem was seen in race terms, whereas in
Ireland and Britain it was seen in class terms.

Treatment of the problem was characterized by usage of the
educational system and was guided by the principle of equality of
opportunity. There was a growing awareness that many ethnic mi-
norities, unwaged working class, and women were being left out of
the educational process and the economic process. It was ascer-
tained that a causal connection existed between the two processes,
that the economically disadvantaged were so because they were
educationally disadvantaged. This led to a focus on educational
underachievement and an array of compensatory policies in Western society aimed directly at those "culturally deprived" within the
educational system. In the United States, the program instigated
was titled "Head Start" and aimed at the pre-school age group. In
Britain, educational priority areas were established. Because the
homes and neighborhoods from which the children came did not
provide enough stimulus for learning, the schools would compen-
sate, particularly at a pre-school stage. The equivalent of these
projects in Ireland is known as the Rutland Street project. The
experiment began in 1969 and ended in 1974; its basic purpose
was to develop strategies to prevent failure at school in disadvantaged areas.

The two main areas that the cultural-deprivation explanation of
school "failure" has focused on for study are language deprivation
and motivation deprivation. Cultural-deprivation theory highlights
"inadequate" parenting, but the "inadequacies" passed on to the
children which were concentrated on were primarily in the area of
language and motivation. Bernstein's work on linguistics examined the linguistic responses given by different social groups (cited in
Gould, 1985).

In his work, Bernstein identified working-class language as a
"restricted code" and middle-class language as an "elaborated

code." The "restricted code" orientates the child toward particular-
istic meanings, whereas the "elaborated code" orientates the child
toward receiving and offering universalistic meanings. The school
is concerned with the latter, and hence the difficulty felt by the
working-class child involved in schooling. Hess and Shipman
(cited in Blackledge & Hunt, 1985) further used Bernstein's work
to emphasize "linguistic deprivation," a concept that Bernstein
himself later strongly repudiated (Bernstein, 1971).

Motivation deprivation focuses on the idea that while the children of the poor are not motivated to learn at school, neither are
they motivated toward achievement, particularly in the area of
work. Characteristics of the culturally deprived were identified by
studies such as that of Passon and Elliot (1968), as follows:

1. language inadequacies;
2. perceptual deficiencies;
3. a mode of expression more rational and concrete than idea-systems-
   focused;
4. an orientation of life that seeks immediate gratification in the here-
   and-now rather than delaying for future advantage;
5. a poor self-image;
6. aspirations too modest for academic success;
7. apathy and detachment from formal goals and processes;
8. limited role-behavior skills and inadequate or inappropriate adult
   models.

The cultural-deprivation theory of educational underachievement implies a deficit approach to working-class culture. A deficit
approach in explaining individual family or community educational deprivation assumes some form of deficiency at the level of
community. It focuses on the unit affected and attempts to find the
cause for the "failure" within it. Thus a structural approach is
neglected, as in genetic theory, and the culture is to some degree
held responsible for failure.

Bernstein's writings are a useful gauge by which to judge how
quickly the emphasis changed from a "deficit" to a "difference"
approach within cultural-deprivation theory. Bernstein attempted

to extricate himself from a "deficit" approach as early as 1969 and
to reinstate his previous work on language within a "difference"
approach. He claims that his descriptive word for working-class
language "restricted code" has been misinterpreted as "linguistic
deprivation" (cited in Rubenstein & Stoneman, 1970).

Bernstein's withdrawal from the "linguistic-deprivation" concept has been followed by a rejection of the "motivation-depriva-
tion" concept on the part of academics. In America, substantial
research on the economically deprived attitude to work has dis-
proved the argument that the unemployed are not motivated to
work. Goodwin in two studies reaches the conclusion that there is
no antiwork ethic or unwillingness to advance apparent (Goodwin,
1970, 1972).

During the late 1960s and early 1970s, the deficit approach
entailed in cultural deprivation theory was strongly criticized
and refuted, particularly in the work (cited in Blackledge & Hunt,
1985) of Reissmann, of Meckler and Gidding, and of Friedenberg
and finally by Nell Keddie (1973). The deficit approach is refuted
on the basis that it is a class-relative perspective and that this
entails a middle-class bias. A difference approach is currently
popular and has emerged in response to such criticisms.

The politics of a cultural-deprivation theory of educational underachievement can be gleaned from the criticisms leveled against
it. First, it implies a deficit approach to the lower socioeconomic
background, or to different racial backgrounds. Second, in em-
bracing the concepts of linguistic and motivation deprivation—
which are, at best, unsound concepts upon which to build a
theory—it attempts to explain away educational underachievement as being something outside the responsibility zone of the
schooling system, or of any of the other systems. Third, its politics
are steeped in a middle-class and white-race location. Its approach
to those who underachieve is neither egalitarian nor respectful but,
rather, is charitable. Thus, once again this is an academic discourse
that contributes to the construction of the early school-leaver in a
subordinate position, in that it looks on them as deficient. It would
seem that proponents of this explanation were and are interested in
social change that would bring about more equal relations, and less
educational subordination on the part of educational underachievers. However, despite this they fall into the political error of com-

bining care with control. They make errors in assessing the needs of others and of how these needs should best be met, in that the underachievers themselves are given no authority or voice. There is evident here a patronizing stance of working for, as opposed to with, people.

A STRUCTURAL DISCOURSE

The explanations of educational failure arising from cultural deprivation theory assume a "problem" approach, wherein reform is possible through small institutional changes, such as "compensatory education." There are also structural explanations of early school-leaving such as theories of direct reproduction. These are more prone to a pessimistic view of the source, extent, and persistence of educational failure. The essential argument of a structuralist approach is that the educational system reproduces the capitalist system and its class relations. The educational system, therefore, institutionalizes and perpetuates inequality. Capitalism does not require everyone to fulfil their educational potential or to become highly qualified and intellectually critical; but people have to be educated just enough to become dutiful workers and consumers. Failure in the educational system is necessary, since not everyone can reach the top stratum in a class society. The majority of the labor force must have limited horizons and limited achievements. In short, they must underachieve.

Most theories of direct reproduction are Marxist in origin. The success of the capitalist systems, according to reproduction theory, depends on two criteria: a generally accepted ideology justifying and legitimating the social order, and a set of "social relationships which both validate this ideology through everyday experience and fragment the ruled into ritually indifferent or antagonistic groups" (Bowles & Gintis, 1976, p. 57). Thus, the maintenance of the capitalist system depends not only on people believing that it is part of the natural order of things, but also on their being accustomed to social relationships that reinforce their beliefs and the purchase of these beliefs in the social world.

According to theories of direct reproduction, education is one of the chief means whereby these tasks are performed. The "educational system is an integral element in the reproduction of the prevailing class structure of society" (Bowles & Gintis, 1976, pp. 125–126). According to this view, reproduction is achieved through two processes: legitimization and socialization. The educational system legitimates the class structure and its inequality by justifying the capitalist ideology of the meritocracy and equal educational opportunity—in Bowles' and Gintis' terms, the "technocratic–meritocratic ideology." It justifies inequalities by perpetuating the belief that the most important positions in society need to be filled by the most talented people, who can be identified through high educational achievement. In undertaking the training, necessary sacrifices are made by these talented people, and rewards in terms of income and prestige are made available to induce them to make these sacrifices. Thus, inequality is presented as being both desirable and necessary. Low educational achievement is thus justifiably rewarded with low income and low status.

The technocratic–meritocratic ideology is criticized as a façade by reproduction theory, on the grounds that the determining factor in educational success is not ability but, rather, socioeconomic background. These theorists argue that this ideological façade camouflages the fact that the educational system functions as a reproductive agent and perhaps as the central agent of direct reproduction.

The concept of socialization as employed by reproduction theorists refers to the process whereby young people are prepared for their place in society by the development in them of the capacities, qualifications, ideas, and beliefs that are appropriate to their position in the capitalist economy. Bowles and Gintis (1976) describe this process as the shaping of the workers' consciousness: "Education tailors the self-concepts, aspirations and social class identifications of individuals to the requirements of the social division of labor" (p. 129).

In brief, the function of education is the reproduction of the capitalist system, and this takes place by means of the legitimization of inequalities through the technocratic–meritocratic ideology associated with capitalism and the socialization of the young into their position in the relations of production.

Bowles and Gintis argue that reproduction is attained by means of the "correspondence principle." This principle refers to the similarities between the social relations of work and the social relations of school: "Specifically the relationship of authority and control between administrators and teachers, teachers and students, and students and their work replicates the hierarchical division of labour which dominates the work place" (Bowles & Gintis, 1976, pp. 11–12). In other words, reproduction is attained not through the curriculum directly but through the hidden curriculum of the school. The correspondence between school relations and work relations has four main aspects:

1. students, like workers, have little power over the process;
2. work and education are both seen as the means to an end, neither of which is intrinsically satisfying but rather undertaken for external rewards and to avoid unpleasant consequences;
3. the division of labor at work is replicated in the compartmentalization of knowledge within the school system;
4. the different "levels" of education correspond to and prepare people for the different "levels" of the occupational structure.

Some of the most influential structuralist writers, such as Althusser, Poulantzas, and Bourdieu, agree on the fundamentals of reproduction theory. These are that education tends to reproduce and legitimate inequalities in wealth and power. They differ, however, in their views on how reproduction occurs. Bourdieu, in particular, differs in the emphasis he places on the importance of "cultural" processes in the maintenance of existing social and economic structures. In his writings, children from the dominant classes are given what he labels "cultural capital" which enables them to acquire qualifications more easily than those without this "cultural capital." He concentrates his attention, however, on third-level students and the university linguistic code for "excellence." Basically, education, as elaborated in Bourdieu's writings, reproduces the class system by conferring status on the children of the dominant classes, because they have "cultural capital." However, no matter what variation one finds in reproduction theories, the central theme remains the same: education directly maintains or reproduces capitalism and its class relations.

In summary, then, a direct theory of reproduction states that the educational system socializes people into the capitalist system and its relations of production, and at the same time legitimates

the system. It does this through a principle of correspondence between the type of schooling each social stratum receives and the
type of employment each stratum is engaged in. It accounts for
educational failure by the fact that because the relations of production are hierarchical, not everyone can reach the top echelons;
educational failure must occur as an integral part of the system
of reproduction. Each social stratum is reproduced through correspondence, and the working class, too, must be reproduced—a
particular type of schooling is implemented to maintain them as
working-class. The low educational qualifications among working-class children channel them toward working-class jobs, and
the high educational qualifications among middle-class children
help them get middle-class jobs.

The main value of reproduction theory is that it looks at the
question of educational failure in its statistical and "objective"
reality, not on an individual level but at a structural level. It con-
veys class structural constraints on early school-leavers. It not
only demonstrates the class basis of educational failure, which is
helpful in the Irish political situation, but shows that failure is not
an educational aberration but, rather, is an intrinsic social function
of education. Therefore, it does not pathologize the question of
early school-leaving; rather, it places it in its structural context.

On the other hand, however, there are serious political drawbacks to this approach. If we take it that there are such objective
laws determining the reality of early school-leaving, we fall into a
modernist trap of believing in the objectivism of the social sciences. Furthermore, there is no active component or agency outside the determining powers of the logic of capital. Despite the fact
that the reproductionist discourse has been successful in challenging the traditional victimological discourses that relate to early
school-leaving by developing insightful theoretical and political
analyses of schooling, its major political failure is, in the words of
theorists Giroux and McLaren, that it fails to "move beyond a
language of critique and domination" (1990, p. 62). They go on
further to explain this political failure in terms of its relevance to
schooling:

> By viewing schooling as primarily reproductive sites, radical
> educators have not been able to develop a theory of schooling

that offers a viable possibility for counterhegemonic struggle and ideological contestation. Within this discourse, schools, teachers, and students are often implicitly viewed as merely extensions of the logic of capital. Instead of grappling with schools as sites of contestation, negotiation, and conflict, radical educators tend to produce an oversimplified version of domination that suggests that schools cannot be seen as sites that offer the possibility of intervention and constructive change. [1990, p. 63]

They argue that reproduction theory fails politically in that it cannot theorize a substantive vision of what should be, that it ignores a theory of ethics, fails to interrogate schools as sites of production, and eradicates any notion of agency on the part of people.

This political critique of reproduction theory is applicable to the question of reproduction theory's relation to early school-leaving. It places early school-leavers in a situation of being structurally determined, and so while the responsibility for their early school-leaving and the consequent subordinate relations suffered does not rest on their shoulders, they are absolutely without power or agency. No attempt is made to theorize how this might be changed or why it should be changed in accordance with ethical referents. This is not just an oversimplification of structural determination; it is fallacious on the basis that people do make history, that they are productive agents. Politically, then, this discourse leaves early school-leavers without a voice, without agency, and so without a struggle. It, in fact, leaves them in a position of bondage to structural determinants.

THE BEGINNINGS OF A POLITICAL DISCOURSE

The explanation of educational failure presented in resistance theory emerges in the literature of the late 1970s and is currently a live theory in the 1990s. It represents a move from traditional and liberal theories of educational underachievement. It emerged in response to what was felt as the overly deterministic aspects of reproduction theory, though it, too, is produced within the Marxist problematic. The concept of resistance attempts to move the emphasis beyond traditional academic analysis to focus on political explanations. Educational underachievement is linked to oppositional behavior, and oppositional behavior is seen to be politically based rather than deviant.

Resistance theory attempts to explain working-class educational underachievement as a political phenomenon. Within resistance theory, working-class children are deemed to recognize the inherent inequalities in the educational system, and because of this knowledge they reject the schooling that they are exposed to. This rejection of schooling is termed working-class resistance. It involves the rejection of school authority by working-class students combined with the rejection of the basic educational paradigm. The ensuing oppositional behavior is responsible for the discipline crisis in working-class schools and is considered a form of class struggle: the working-class children's rejection of middle-class education. In resisting the aims and values of schooling, working-class children fail themselves.

Resistance theory is a qualification of reproduction theories, the deterministic elements being replaced by more voluntarist elements. Regarding the acceptance of low-paid manual work by working-class people who resist education, there is seen to be a correspondence between counter-school culture and working-class culture, in particular the factory shop-floor culture (Willis, 1977). The correspondence between the oppositional behavior involved in the counter-school culture and the oppositional behavior involved on the factory-floor gives them the confidence in their labor-market position to enable them to reject their schooling. So, in effect, resistance theory is basically a more voluntarist form of social reproduction theory, which provides a mixture of political and cultural explanations for working-class underachievement. Theoretical arguments of resistance theory draw heavily upon the work of radical ethnographers. In particular the empirical studies of Paul Willis (1977) and Angela McRobbie (1980), both from the Centre for Contemporary Cultural Studies at the University of Birmingham, are cited.

The earliest and most influential of these ethnographies—and the one that can best be gleaned for the political implications of resistance theory—is *Learning to Labour*, by Paul Willis (1977), which presents the outcome of his research. Using an ethnographic model, Willis studied twelve working-class pupils in a working-class school in a working-class town, who readily displayed

oppositional behavior to the schooling system. He followed their
progress from school into the labor market, pursuing what is basically a reproduction-type model. His concern was to explain "why
working-class children got working-class jobs." His explanation
of this phenomenon brought resistance theory to the fore in the
study of the education system.

His arguments for resistance fall into two parts. Firstly, counter-
school culture, characterized by resistance and opposition to authority, is an aspect of working-class culture. Counter-school
culture is one expression of certain basic working-class attitudes
and values. Resistance and oppositional culture will always
emerge in schools where working-class pupils attend because of
the pupils' working-class roots. Secondly, there is a similarity or
correspondence between the counter-school culture and the factory shop-floor culture, which makes the transition from school to
work easy. It is the cultural background of the students which
prepares them for factory work.

Willis' work focuses on the oppositional behavior of the counter-school subculture he presents. The oppositional behavior of the
subculture's members involves opposition to school authority, to
the timetable imposed on them, and to the curriculum they are
supposed to be involved in. There is a recognition by the resisting
pupils that the members of the staff are enemies, that they have
authority that they use unfairly and unsparingly, and that the authorities expect that the pupils submit. This is met by the insubor-
dination of the "lads." The teachers and what they teach is rejected
and challenged in countless ways by the subculture. "Dossing,"
"blagging," and "wagging" are the terms used by the "lads" to
describe how they simply do not conform to what is demanded
from them by the formal schooling system. They limit the demands made on them to an absolute minimum—for example, not
even writing as much as their name for months at a time. "Having a
laff" is the chief employment and the informal reaction of the gang
as they pass their days in opposition to the schooling system.

Willis argues that the counter-school culture entails an important "penetration" of the conditions of working-class life. According to Willis, the subculture does not accept the educational
paradigm that insists that if you work hard enough and have some
ability, you will achieve educational qualifications followed by

financial and social rewards. The "lads" see that "a few can make it, the class can never follow" (Willis, 1977, p. 128). This understanding is a working-class understanding of their social position. Therefore, they do not participate in trading respect and obedience for knowledge and hoped-for qualifications. Willis regards this as a "radical act: it refuses to collude in its own educational suppression" (Willis, 1977, p. 128). Because of this, the concept of "resistance" is introduced since the "lads" oppositional behavior is considered a radical act. Also, the term resistance is considered appropriate because this radical act is based on a working-class penetration of the educational paradigm, which brings about working-class educational suppression. The oppositional behavior to the school system is seen as emancipatory in that there is a class resistance, in an area of recognized class conflict, to the educational suppression of the working class.

The movement of these young people who resist education into unskilled and semi-skilled jobs occurs in two ways. Firstly, by their resistance to the schooling system they have, ironically enough, limited themselves rather than freed themselves, according to Willis. He considers their resistance as "no more than a momentary glimpse of freedom"; they now have no choice but to slot into unskilled and semiskilled work because of their educational failure. Their resistance has actually served the reproductive process, relegating working-class children to working-class occupations. Secondly, it is the working-class background and its culture that is the educator of the resistance. Their familiarity with the factory-floor culture, and the conditions of employment within it, gives the "lads" the confidence in their labor position which enables them to forgo their educational chances.

Echoing reproduction theory, Willis argues that a correspondence exists between oppositional behavior in school and the concurrent minimization of the demands of the school authorities on the counter-school culture, on the one hand, and the oppositional behavior in the factory and the concurrent minimization of the demands of the factory management on the working-classes, on the other. This continuity between the factory-floor culture and the counter-school culture is, according to Willis, the second reason why working-class children get working-class jobs.

Evidently, Willis' work is not just an argument for reproduction theory, but an in-depth study of how that reproduction process operates for working-class children. He concludes that the process involves a form of resistance to schooling on the pupils' part, because of their working-class insights into the inequalities of the educational system, which brings about their educational failure. However, resistance is clearly bound to the Marxist reproductionist problematic in that Willis considers it to be based on "merely a momentary glimpse of freedom." It is not based on a clearly worked out emancipatory struggle, but on a reaction to what is after all only "a partial penetration" of the terms of subordination. Nonetheless, educational failure is brought into the political arena by this conclusion.

The political advantages of resistance theory are that it at least leaves us with a sense of a struggle being waged. It presents some possible political explanations as to why working-class children underachieve at school, drop out of school, and accept low-paid work. Within this approach early school-leavers are, to some extent, seen as thinking agents in that they recognize that the educational system has stacked the odds against their succeeding and that it does not promote their advancement but their subordination, and they reject it. Their working-class background is seen as a site of cultural production in that it familiarizes them with factory-floor oppositional behavior and the limiting of the demands by management on their time and energy. Willis argues that working-class children are also thinking subjects because they can translate this into limiting the demands of the schooling system on their time; they choose to underachieve, and his study operates to give them a voice. They are also theorized as active subjects in that they choose to leave school early because of their confidence in their labor-market position and their feeling that the schooling system is irrelevant to the achievement of their labor position.

However, the political drawbacks to resistance theory are also numerous. It remains trapped in the binary opposition of reproduction/resistance analysis. Resistance is almost totally reduced to a cultural process of reproduction in the sense that all that can be achieved within its theoretical parameters is the furtherance of capitalist reproduction. Power is still overwhelmingly on the side of the structural forces, reducing struggle to resistance as opposed to a more transformative type of action. Marxist in its problematic, it focuses overwhelmingly on class struggle as the only form of political struggle. Much of the political critique leveled earlier at reproduction theory can also be applied to resistance theory, in that it does not afford us a transformative or ethical version of what could or should be. Though it certainly draws a more politically enabling picture of early school-leavers, and does not construct them in positions of subordination, it leaves them without a political strategy or political project for emancipatory social change.

This chapter has viewed theoretical discursive constructions that relate to early school-leavers, mining these constructions for their political implications for the social position of these school-leavers. I argue that some of them discursively construct and facilitate the material construction of early school-leavers in subordinate positions, by theorizing the early school-leavers as genetically or culturally deficient. Reproduction theory, while not directly constructing early school-leavers as being deficient, maintains the issue outside the terrain of political struggle. Resistance theory, on the other hand, brings the issue into the political terrain, but the struggle is presented as being doomed to failure. These varying discourses, to greater or lesser extents, mark serious exclusionary or negative inclusionary discursive relations.

Yet, it is evident that early school-leavers occupy relations of subordination that warrant the articulation of early school-leaving as being a terrain of political struggle, and the articulation of the subordinate relations that early school-leavers live under as being relations of oppression. Once this political space or crisis is acknowledged, is it possible to begin to develop strategies that move toward the challenging of, and transformation of, the material and discursive crisis of the space of early school-leavers? This work moves on in the belief that it is not only possible but necessary.

5

A Reproduction/Resistance
Reading

The history of knowledge would lead us to be wary of simply discarding old knowledge just because it is subject to criticism. Therefore, while I have argued that reproduction and resistance theories are limited academic narratives, nevertheless they are important enough to merit detailed consideration. This chapter examines the extent to which they are progressive in terms of transformative political practice, insofar as they both represent an important moment in identifying the dominant class ideological interests at work in the schooling situation. To reveal the strengths of this approach, in this chapter I carry out a reproduction/resistance reading of the conversational text in Part I. Here the reader can merge or contrast her or his interpretations of the earlier conversations with a theoretical analysis.

To do these reproduction/resistance readings, it is historically and conceptually appropriate to work temporarily within a modernist social-research framework. From this perspective, the conversations of Chapters 1, 2, and 3 become qualitative data, "in-depth discussions," which were collected through the use of research instruments such as "participant observation" and "in-depth discussioning." I become an objective social scientist reporting my findings from my field work. In this framework, the reading must become a "rational," "objective," "factual" account, and other readings (including yours and mine) would not be as "true," "correct," or insightful as this one. Within this social research framework, the project is to uncover rules about how society and its systems operate—in this particular case, how early school-leaving occurs systematically. Having set this social research framework, let me proceed with a standard reproductionist reading.

A REPRODUCTION ANALYSIS

Reproduction theory specifies that educational underachievement among the working class is a structural reality of the schooling system. It is argued that the schooling system maintains and reproduces the capitalist system and its class relations of production. The schooling system under the influence of the economic system is said to replicate the class system. Schooling is one of the means by which the working-class, middle-class, and ruling-class positions are maintained. It achieves this reproduction of classes through several ways: the most important way is through limiting the achievements of certain strata and ensuring that they underachieve with regard to educational qualifications. Failure is necessary in the educational system to slot people into their class position. Not everyone can succeed educationally, or there would be too many in the top echelons of the hierarchy.

The schooling system is said to achieve this replication through the principle of correspondence. The type of schooling each stratum receives corresponds to the type of employment each stratum is placed in. The working class then receive a particular type of schooling that affirms them in a working-class position in the labor force; schooling directs them toward low educational qualification, which leads to low wages. Educational failure is thus an integral part of working-class schooling, according to reproduction theory.

The conversations in Part I are about collective or individualistic presentations of identities, and the analysis can only be derived from the school-leavers' (perceived or semi-perceived) understanding of the impact of the system on their life path. Reproduction theory, on the other hand, is a structural theory with deterministic tendencies and presents us with a structural picture of how the educational system eliminates the early school-leaver. The application of reproduction theory to this data cannot lead to a total explanation of early school-leaving, yet it can convey structural trends. In particular, it can highlight the educational system's part in encouraging or determining early school-leaving among those from lower socioeconomic backgrounds.

To apply a reproduction analysis is to locate the extent to which the educational system imposes itself on the early school-leavers to bring about the end result of underachievement and early school-leaving. Did their schooling control and manipulate their underachievement? If one pursues the correspondence between educational exclusion and labor-market exclusion, one must disclose the importance of the educational system in the socialization of the young people into nonparticipation.

The young people's dynamic presentation of the causes of their early school-leaving and underachievement revolves around their rejection of the school system. The question that is posed by reproduction theory and the correspondence principle is upon what aspect of the educational system is this rejection based? What do they outline as the facets of the educational system that they reacted against? What were the processes used by the educational system that brought about consequences of reaction and rejection as related by the young people?

The findings of this research indicate that the educational system worked in several ways to effect the elimination of these young people. Firstly, through a process of streaming, pupils were placed in low-grade classes where containment, as opposed to learning, appears to have been implemented. Secondly, the curriculum was considered to be meaningless to the young people, and their schooling did not educate them to the relevance of the curriculum and, in particular, to the connection between educational qualifications and their labor-market position. There was little either in the way of sympathy or empathy between the teachers and the young people from lower socioeconomic backgrounds. Finally, absenteeism was ignored, if not indeed to some extent encouraged.

Low-Grade Classes

The educational system streams children into groups of high achievers and low achievers on the basis of IQ and performance. Before second-level education starts, the young people are allocated to low-grade classes. Once inside these low-grade classes, the young people quickly realize that they are in "a class for messers," as they see it. The young people claim that no effort was made to teach them once placed in one of these classes. They react to a situation where they feel they are being "put to the ground," and they have significant peer support in this reaction. Thus containment and discipline are the main elements on the classroom agenda. The curriculum can no longer be used for mediation, because the young people know that they have been excluded from the mainstream examination process.

The lower the class grade, the more uncontrollable were the young people. Note how in the description of their schooling experience the young people repeatedly stated that "messing" was what they believed school was for. Take Margo's and Michael's comments, for example; Margo states, "That's what I thought school was for, messing," and Michael states that even when he wanted to concentrate in his class, there could have been no possibility because the "blokes" were nothing but a "crowd of messers."

They feel they were given nothing to do, they were constantly bored, and there was a total lack of teaching ability on the part of the teachers. The general feeling is that they were taught nothing in school. This could be attributed as part of their conflict with, and hostility toward, the teachers, were it not for the fact that evidence of nonteaching is in abundance. The majority of the young people, due to no physical disability whatever, were below their age group's literacy and numeracy levels. The final indictment of the schooling system as being non-educational for these young people is that they leave school with severe literacy problems. Take Dave's final words on his schooling experience: he states he cannot read, or at least he could not until he was given literacy classes having left school. Not only, then, are they excluded from the educational qualifications such as Group, Intermediate, and Leaving Certificate examinations, but they are actually excluded from the most basic elements of education—reading and writing.

The Meaninglessness of the Curriculum

Applying reproduction theory uncovers a second way in which the educational system brings about the educational underachievement of the early school-leavers—it is through the nonmotivation of these young people. The curriculum is seen by the kids to be utterly irrelevant. They explain that they felt no interest in the curriculum, and for the most part none was generated by the teachers. They repeatedly say they do not know why they were studying the curriculum, and they did not see its relevance. In retrospect, when meeting the impossibility of finding employment without educational qualification, some have found out for themselves that there is a basic link between qualifications and attaining work. Others deny the existence of this link, even in retrospect, because they see people of Leaving Certificate standard who are unemployed or who accept badly paid service jobs.

From a structural point of view, it is clear that the educational system is not successful (though attempts are made) in imparting knowledge concerning the vital link between high educational qualifications, high-status work, and high financial income, even though the schooling system does attempt to. When the educational system fails to direct itself toward educating the young people to this link, it allows them to perceive schooling as irrelevant. By not fulfilling this crucial role of education, it is left to the family to direct the young people toward considering the link between educational qualifications and career paths. In the families of these young people from lower socioeconomic backgrounds, the knowledge simply was not there to explain effectively why educational qualifications were so important. These young people are finding out too late. Judy expresses how the link between school and work was not made clear to her.

Judy: I think our parents have a lot to do with it. Like the time we were young, ye know teaching ye to understand like the reasons why we have to go to school, why it's important to learn things.

HF: Do you think your parents were good or bad at teaching you that?

Judy: I wouldn't say they were bad, but they weren't good, like, when you were younger, we weren't really told that school is all that

important. We were told to go alright, but they don't tell you any of
the reasons as to why the exams are important.

HF: And why do you think exams are important now?

Judy: You go to school to learn. You want to get a good job. You need
to pass the exam, so you need to learn but you don't understand that
when you're young. . . . Nobody would explain it to you. Teachers
should explain it, like why you're doing your exams and all. . . . Me
da would have liked me to stay. He wanted me to do my Leaving and
all like, but none of these explanations, why, ye know.

These young people are interested in earning money since they
are from backgrounds of financial deprivation and they have a
high respect for hard work, but the educational system does not
make explicit the link between the school and the labor market,
and so the curriculum is perceived to be irrelevant to them. Thus
they are simply not motivated by the educational system and feel
that it is possible to drop out of school without any repercussions
for their labor market position.

There is a second reason why the curriculum is seen as meaningless by these young people. Being part of a community and
family of the lower socioeconomic strata, their experience and
perception of work has culturally been limited to that of unemployment or manual work. They are culturally given a respect for
manual work; not to have this respect would be to debase, or
downgrade, their own family and community. Because they are
part of the lower socioeconomic strata, the young people are particularly sensitive and vulnerable to downgrading. Thus there is a
strong orientation toward and appreciation of manual work combined with a limited perspective of manual work as the only type
of work there is. This was amply displayed in their attitude toward
white-collar work. However, in contrast to this, the curriculum and
examinations are completely geared toward white-collar work.
Thus, the curriculum is divorced from the reality of working young
people. They would not see a link between the curriculum and
work, because work means manual work to them and there is no
link made between the curriculum and manual work. There is no
evidence to suggest that the educational system has bridged this
gap or made the curriculum relevant to these young people. By not
using the life experience of the young people as a basis from which

to educate, and by not linking the background of the young people to the curriculum, the curriculum is irrelevant and meaningless. This lack of relevance and lack of meaning of the curriculum can be seen as a structural cause of the young people's underachievement.

Lack of Identification of Teachers with Young People from a Lower Socioeconomic Background

It has been pointed out that the curriculum is responsible to a certain degree for the minimal school participation of the early school-leavers in that it does not take into account the particular circumstances of those from lower socioeconomic backgrounds. Insofar as teachers are the representatives of the educational system and, as described by Freire in *Pedagogy of the Oppressed* (1972), "depositors" of the curriculum, it follows that they might not be sensitive or knowledgeable regarding a lower socioeconomic background. This research gives evidence not just of a lack of identification but of severe conflict between teachers and students; this conflict is described later in this chapter, since it is particularly relevant to resistance theory.

The greatest evidence for nonidentification on the part of the teachers with those from lower socioeconomic backgrounds, however, is not given in relation to the young people themselves. A hierarchical relationship between student and teacher usually causes conflict regardless of the social background factor. In any hierarchy, discontent emanates from the individual at the lower position in the hierarchy. The school situation does not differ. However, not only pupil/teacher conflict is reported, but parent/teacher conflict. Important evidence regarding nonidentification and insensitivity to those from the lower socioeconomic strata is to be found in relation to the interaction between the parents and the teachers. In every case of conflict between the schooling system and the young person, the parents went to the teacher to resolve the problem or at least to keep their child in school. Each time the conflict heightened, particularly when the father entered the interaction, and the end result was the parent removing their child from school. In the case of Margo and Jackie, the parents could not afford to buy a school coat for their twin daughters. After much delay, the mother went up to explain, but no understanding came about. Next, the father went to the school to explain, or more probably to defend his children, and the outcome was disastrous for the children in that they had to leave school. It would seem that the teachers made even less headway in relating to the parents where no hierarchical conflict should have been apparent. The frequency of breakdown in relations between the teachers and parents, and the basis of the conflict, suggests and substantiates a lack of identification on the teachers' part to the pupils' circumstances. This breakdown in relations, the teachers' class position, and their distance from the low financial and social status brings about in its own way the exclusion from the school system of those from lower socioeconomic backgrounds.

Encouragement of Nonparticipation

To complete the framework of a structural dimension to the exclusion of the lower socioeconomic backgrounds from the schooling process, we need to examine the reaction of the schooling system to the non-participation of its clients. The subjects of this research indicate that the response of the schools to their nonparticipation was ambiguous to say the least.

There were many levels at which the young people did not participate in school: for example, not studying particular subjects such as English or Math, which are essential to acquiring any educational standard or qualification and are particularly relevant to everyday social skills and interaction in general. Sometimes the young person would dislike a subject or perhaps just "mess" in a particular class, so much that the teacher would refuse to teach them. Thus the teacher collaborated in the pupils' exclusion from essential subjects.

At another level, in reaction to conflict between teacher and pupil, the pupil would "bunk off" from those particular classes. Conflicts would not be resolved, and the teacher, probably with twenty-nine other people she or he identified as being uninterested in the subject matter, would be aware that one or more pupils were "bunking off." Gemma explains how the teacher would know she was "bunking off" but "would not care."

Gemma: They wouldn't come for you. They just do that. They didn't want us in the class because they knew we weren't working for them.

"Bunking off" then removed the young person from an intolerable situation, and in turn an intolerable situation was removed from the classes, from the teacher's point of view.

HF: Would they notice you were gone?

Joe: There was a teacher who knew I bunked off, the English teacher. She'd say, "You're not going down the river today again," but she didn't care.

HF: Would you say that happens—like if you cause trouble at school that they don't care whether you're there or you're not there.

Joe: Sometimes they don't. Some of them do.

On another level, outside the individual teacher's area of responsibility, young people went "on the hop" and "took" days off to such an extent that they barely knew what the different subjects were. This absenteeism was obviously noticed, yet it continued practically unchallenged. In effect the system turns a blind eye to absenteeism among those from lower socioeconomic backgrounds. Obviously, the problem is so pervasive, and indeed structural, that to tackle it would be to call the whole educational system into question. However, in relation to this research it is clear that the educational system colludes with these young people's nonparticipation on different levels—opting out of particular classes and nonattendance during a considerable number of school days. It colludes in it in that it is aware of working-class absenteeism but does not deal with it.

There is one aspect of the findings of this research that deviates from the exact particulars of reproduction theory. Reproduction theory states that the forces of reproduction are linked in particular to the economic system, that the labor market has an impact on the form of schooling given to a particular stratum. However, the information here in addition to conveying the reproductive tendencies of the educational system shows that the economic system has a direct impact on the young people's decision to leave school. The economic system not only influences the educational system but, more directly, makes an impression on the young people's early school-leaving and life path. The labor market acts as a direct pulling force.

Economic Inducement

A crucial feature of life in the lower socioeconomic strata is poverty in its crudest financial form. The young people talk about lack of money at home when questioned directly. They obviously have no access to money themselves except through illegal channels. They are reared in the context of family and neighborhood unemployment. The majority of parents were, at the time of the research, dependent on social welfare. Low financial income is the norm. Even if one parent is employed, what employment there is tends to be part-time manual work or temporary seasonal work. Due to the very fact of belonging to the lower socioeconomic strata and having to cope on a daily basis with lack of finances, there is continuous pressure to obtain an income. The young people outline adequately their wish for an independent income, their respect for money, and, furthermore, how they contributed to the family income and, in point of fact, how they were obligated to contribute to the family finances. While parents seemed to want their children to stay in school, once the young person had come to want to leave school, finding work was obviously a viable and welcome alternative for the parents. Having had no money for themselves previously, the young person is obviously very anxious to acquire some.

Judy: Like, say, I wouldn't have got that job, I would have had to stay in school. I wouldn't have anything for myself. I'd still be sponging [unfairly extracting money or goods] off my Ma and Da.

On the other hand, the economic structures of capitalism need to maintain the lower socioeconomic strata. Unemployment is a structural reality of the market system, and low-paid temporary workers are essential for particular positions in the labor market. The labor market in this particular area required early school-leavers for the unskilled factory labor. Judy states that all the factories employed people as young and unqualified as she. However, this work was temporary, and the young people were always likely to be laid off. Other factory work was seasonal, such as fish-factory work, which also needed temporary and unqualified workers. In short, a labor market was there for these young people. Due to their state of low finance and their aspirations simply to attain work and finance, they were obviously vulnerable to slot into this labor market niche. If in no other way, this can be seen geographically from the positioning of the factories in close proximity to large-scale public estates. This niche in the labor market is reserved for young people of this socioeconomic background, and indeed those positions look extremely attractive to those whose aspirations are to have an independent income as early as possible. The temporary nature of this work, its vulnerability to slumps in the market, and its low pay are far from the minds of the young people. It is only when they face unemployment and are unqualified that they realize they have been channeled into the life path that will maintain them in the lower socioeconomic strata.

This economic inducement from the labor market has the power to attract young people from lower socioeconomic backgrounds. It leads them to leave school early, as can be seen from the fact that every early school-leaver left school to find employment and to contribute to the family income. In a very practical way, the economic system imposes its force, to reproduce the lower socioeconomic strata, directly on the young people.

A RESISTANCE ANALYSIS

Resistance theory presents educational underachievement among working-class people as a political and cultural response to middle-class schooling. Oppositional behavior among schoolgoers is said to be informed by a working-class understanding that the system perpetuates inequalities against them. On the basis of this understanding, they reject the school authority and resist the aims and values of schooling. Educational underachievement comes about because in engaging in resistance to schooling, they avoid participation and so fail themselves. The acceptance of low-paid work in the labor market is then facilitated by the correspondence between the counter-school culture and the factory-floor culture, both being oppositional to authority. In addition, their confidence in their labor-market position makes it possible for the working class to reject schooling.

It is this working-class resistance to schooling that brings about their educational underachievement. Because of this underachievement at school and the consequent lack of educational qualifications, they condemn themselves to futures of low-paid manual work. Working-class resistance to education, then, in effect plays its part in the reproductive process of the capitalist system. In resisting and rejecting their schooling, working-class schoolgoers perpetuate their manual laboring positions. Their resistance relegates them to working-class positions.

Resistance theory is essentially a reworking of reproduction theory, softening the determinism of reproduction in favor of a more voluntaristic interpretation. In claiming that working-class educational underachievement is part of an overall framework of resistance, it directs attention away from the imposition by the education system of "failure" on the young people, and it concentrates on the young people's response to schooling. It focuses on the actual process of educational underachievement and early school-leaving from the point of view of the working class. It presents responses of cultural creativity by the young people to the structural constraints of their schooling

The application of resistance theory to this research is limited in one aspect. While the focus is on working-class resistance to their educational suppression, the subjects of this research come from the working class certainly, but from the lower socioeconomic background—from what can be termed as the unwaged working class. Employment is their aim, but unemployment is the reality of their family's economic status and regular experience in their communities. For the most part, the findings of this research—the presentation of the young people's schooling experience and the process of their early school-leaving—converge with the findings of resistance theory. However, there are also important points of difference. The following pages examine the points of convergence and divergence.

The application of resistance theory to the findings of this research follows. Analysis is possible by discussing the major points of contact and divergence between the findings here and the arguments postulated by Willis (1977). Divergences emerge partially due to the differences in the subjects' backgrounds. Overall, however, evidence emerges that supports a resistance theory of the reactive type rather than of an emancipatory type. Without quite proving a class consciousness, there is evidence of class conflict. The analysis proceeds by discussing the young people's consciousness of the suppression of their class by the educational system and its methods of ensuring subordination. The basis and method of their rejection of school is examined. Finally, a cultural reaction to their class status is described.

A Partial Penetration of Their Educational Suppression

Resistance theory explains educational underachievement by arguing that working-class young people recognize that the educational system has stacked the odds against their success. They recognize that the educational system is not for their advancement, but a method of subordination. The preceding section on reproduction adequately describes how the educational system brought about the educational underachievement of the early school-leavers. This information shows the extent to which the young people understood the invidious nature of the schooling system. They believed that they were simply not being educated in school—in particular, that they were not being taught because they were streamed into classes outside the examination process. Insofar as there was an attempt to teach them, the curriculum was irrelevant. They believe that they were not exposed to the connection between educational qualifications and employment and that the curriculum was not going to teach them what they wanted to know. So school for the young people was intolerable. The findings support resistance theory at this point. However, they do not support Willis' view of a penetration of the educational paradigm, a realization that a few of the working-class pupils can get through the system but "the class can never follow" (Willis, 1977, p. 128). There was no such class penetration of the educational paradigm evident. Only the reality of their individual experience was expressed by the young people, and this reality was expressed as the educational system being intolerable for them individually. In fact, the education system was criticized because it did not make the link between educational qualifications and the labor market. This only became apparent to young people when potential employers asked for their qualifications.

The findings of this research, then, do not support a working-class partial penetration of the educational paradigm. The early school-leavers, however, did have a substantial and discriminating understanding of the way in which the school brought about or was responsible for their individual educational underachievement and their educational suppression. Thus the findings support the element of resistance theory that states that the working class recognize that the educational system is not there for their advancement.

A Method of Subordination

Resistance theory argues that the education system is recognized by the young people as a means of subordinating the working class rather than as a means of their advancement. The results of this research show that the young people recognized that schooling was a method of subordination. This is reflected in their attitude of extreme hostility toward school. Even those who have subsequently realized the importance of qualifications will study for examinations at night in their own time, but they will not return to school. Their schooling experience has been a most unhappy one.

One of the chief methods of subordination recognized by the young people is to be found in teacher/pupil relations. The teacher represents the schooling system for the young people, and, insofar as they understood their subordination, they pointed to the teachers as its primary agents. Basically, each individual recognized that a submissive attitude was required on his or her part. The hierarchical relations in the schooling system between teacher and pupil always demand submissiveness on the part of the pupils. However, the pupil/teacher relationship in the working-class schools as described by the early school-leavers was deeply marred by open conflict. The young people regard the teachers as an oppositional entity insofar as they represent the schooling system and that they require a submissive attitude on the part of the pupils. The pupils do not see that the submissive attitude is required for a smooth process of learning, since they do not acknowledge that any teaching process is occurring. They refuse to be submissive to teachers in incidents of conflict because they simply do not respect the teachers as teachers; they do not consider that they are being taught anything.

There is another dimension to this conflict in which the pupils refuse to behave respectfully toward the teacher: their experience of schooling has made them feel that the teachers have no respect for them. Margo explains that she would have respect for the teachers if they had respect for her.

HF: Did you not have respect for the teachers, or what?

Margo: I would, but they never have. Most of the teachers up in Scoil don't have respect for you. Like they say anything to you: "Get out of this bleeding class." The others [teachers] wouldn't give a shit.

Because of the feeling that the teachers have no respect for them and treat them unfairly, they see that their submissiveness is required as part of a discriminatory suppression. They believe teachers were continuously "moaning at" them and treating them "like dirt."

Mairead: They thought he's the teacher and that's it and he's over us and that's it, he's going to boss us around and we have to let him. No way, I wouldn't let anyone stand all over me. Like he was really standing on them. He was walking them into the ground, he was.

It is evident from the strength of the reaction that these young people see the teacher's behavior as oppressive and that they feel a need to defend themselves. They recognize that the power is on the teachers' side in the conflict—and it is usually this very power over them that they react against—but they do not see why the teachers deserve this power since they claim that no teaching process occurs. Gemma and Margo separately state that it was their lack of submissiveness that got them "thrown out" of school. They both felt that had it been possible for them to have "kept their mouths shut" or to have let the teacher have "the last say," they could have progressed in school because their academic records were acceptable.

While the young people recognize that a submissive attitude was required from them, they interpret this as a discriminatory action on the part of those who represent the schooling system. This they feel particularly antagonistic toward, because they fiercely believe and try to prove through examples that school taught them nothing.

Rejecting School

The next point made by resistance theory is that due to the recognition that school suppresses the working class, they reject school by engaging in oppositional behavior and in so doing bring about their own educational failure.

The findings of this research show that the young people blamed their educational underachievement on their nonparticipation or minimal participation in school, as opposed to lack of "intelligence." Through their non-participation in an irrelevant and boring curriculum, they were simply reacting to a nonteaching process and to teachers who demanded their submissiveness or even subordination and who did not deserve their respect. Thus, the political interpretation of educational underachievement, rather than the pathological interpretation, is obviously supported by the experience of schooling as understood by the early school-leavers.

The basis on which they rejected school can be divided into three aspects. They firstly reject school on the basis that there was a lack of a teaching process and the teachers could not or would not educate them. Secondly, they reject school because the curriculum was seen to be irrelevant to them. Thirdly, they reject the authority of the teacher, because they understood that authority was being used against them unfairly. They believed that the teachers had no respect for them and so felt the need to defend themselves.

The rejection of school on the basis of a lack of a real teaching process and of the teachers' inability or neglect of their education deviates from the emphasis of its rejection by Willis' working-class "lads." The point of view of the early school-leavers, as expressed by Cyril—"Because we weren't getting our education right"—points more to an emphasis on reproduction theory and to a correspondence between exclusion from the educational process and exclusion from the labor force. Thus, two out of the three reasons for why they reject school are supportive of resistance theory. The young people's nonparticipation tends to be based on mere reaction, as is their oppositional behavior. The degree to which the young peoples' oppositional behavior causes their educational underachievement is more limited than in the resistance model, in that the educational system ensured their failure by streaming them and by not engaging them in an educational process. Thus their rejection of school is in direct reaction to the conditions of schooling. This finding represents a slight change in emphasis from Willis' argument, in that structural constraints are emphasized, to a greater degree than cultural creativity, as the basis for resistance.

Oppositional Behavior

Resistance theory postulates that the young people engage in oppositional behavior and in doing so bring about their own educational failure. The findings of this research support this hypothesis and indicate that there is a continuum of oppositional behavior in operation. At one end of the continuum there is oppositional behavior that maintains itself within the framework of the schooling system and simply upholds the minimal or non-participation of the pupils such as "messing" and "bunking off," until it is possible for them legally to reject school finally. At the other end of the continuum there is a violent reaction to what is considered the repression of the school. There is a violent response by the young men on both an individual level and a group level, which is destructive to the school and its teachers and is described by the early school-leavers as "running amuck." This violent and destructive reaction is a response to socioeconomic suppression among young men. It cannot always be contained within the schooling system, which indeed exacerbates the situation, and which on occasion faces what is tantamount to rioting violence.

The stories told by Joe and Jim are evidence of individual conflict with violence. Both young men claim that the violence was initiated by the teacher.

Joe: We'd be messing because we were bored, and the teacher would hit you and you'd hit them back and all.

H: Did you hit the teacher back?

Joe: Once I did.

Violence is something to which the young men have a learned and decisive answer: they react instantly and destructively.

Jim: He hit me once, but I levelled him out of it.

H: What way did he hit you?

Jim: A hard T-square, he gave me a belt of it, and I hit the chair off his head.

Violent reactions are not limited to the individual and cannot be treated as individual pathological or psychopathic reactions. In discussions with Eamonn, Cyril, and Dave, they describe a group violent outburst directed against the school.

[In a group discussion]

Cyril: Yeah, the whole bleeding school went mad. We were all going to bash the masters one by one. All the fifth and sixth years all around shouting, "One two three four, what the fucking hell is this?" Now we were all running around jumping off the stairs and all, kicking the windows through and all. Fucking great it was, ran amuck we did.

This oppositional behavior is quite aside from the type of oppositional behavior described by Willis as bringing about their educational underachievement. This is an angry, violent, and destructive action with roots not just in suppression by the educational system, but suppression in all social and economic life. This is a reaction after the suppression has done its damage, not a reaction based on emancipatory interests. This information then reduces the evidence of the young people having a momentary glimpse of freedom as described by Willis. There is resistance evident, but the forces of suppression here had their influence, and a strained, angry, destructive violence emerges. This resistance is not, in the short term, emancipatory.

A Cultural Insight to Rebel against Inequality

Resistance theory links into reproduction theory by describing the correspondence between the oppositional school culture and the oppositional factory-floor culture. This correspondence is not to be found among the subjects of this study, all of whom are from the lowest socioeconomic strata, are largely excluded from the labor market, and are dependent on subsistence financing from the state. As stated in the previous section, the most obvious correspondence is their exclusion or suppression through both the educational and the economic system. The roots of their oppositional behavior, then, does not arrive from a correspondence to factory-floor culture.

Willis argues that the working-class background gave the "kids" the insight to rebel against overt inequality regarding their school position. To a certain extent this is also reflected in the findings of this research. However, the word "insight" is not appropriate within the terms of the findings. It does not take great acumen on the part of the young people to recognize inequality when they come from lower socioeconomic backgrounds. This "insight" is a reality of their everyday life that they cannot avoid. Their cultural background gives them an awareness and sensitivity rather than an insight into their suppression, or, as they say, "being put down." They constantly feel the need to defend themselves.

[From my diary]

> One of the trainees described the young people's reaction on going into town today. She explains how they react on going into another class area such as Grafton Street. "It's like they react to these f . . . . . . posh b . . . ." She says the young people actually group together for protection, almost. They freeze. When I asked her why, she said I should see the way people react to them. As soon as they hear they're from _____, "They do not want to know us." She said, "I think a lot of them feel put down even before they start. They're made to feel working-class, they're made to feel small."

Therefore, unlike the results of Willis' research, the findings of this research point not to an "insight to rebel against overt inequality," but to a learned defensive sensitivity and wariness to being

"put down" by anyone and everyone. Their cultural background
then gives them the need, or else they feel the need to defend
themselves constantly. This accounts partially for their individual
overt reaction against the teachers' demands for submissiveness
and the young people's understanding that they are being "put
down" or "walked on" by the teachers. Their difficulty with the
teachers is probably heightened by the fact that teachers represent
a different class from them and, furthermore, a class that in the
hierarchical relations is a step higher than they are.

That their cultural background gives them the awareness to defend themselves or fight for themselves can be seen from the interaction between the parents and the teachers. These relations
mirrored those of the teachers and students in that they usually
deteriorated into direct and open conflict. When the mother failed
in negotiations for her child, the father went to the school. If he felt
an injustice was being perpetrated against his child or felt that the
child was being "put down" by the teacher, aggression overflowed.
The young people's sensitivity to their class position is to some
degree responsible for their oppositional behavior toward schooling authorities, but this is not to say that their sensitivity is not
related to the reality of their treatment due to their class position.
Their sensitivity allows them to be acutely aware of the extent to
which they are being excluded from the educational process.

Confidence in the Labor Market

Resistance theory finally suggests that working-class pupils leave
school early or reject school, since a correspondence exists between counter-school oppositional culture and factory-floor culture; this correspondence gives them confidence in their
labor-market position and gives them the belief that the schooling
system is irrelevant to the achievement of that position.

Since the subjects of this research come from the lower socioeconomic backgrounds, the findings once again do not fully support this view. Certainly a driving force for the young people to
leave school was that they felt the curriculum was irrelevant for
working-class positions, which was the only perspective they had
on work. However, there was a sense that, in retrospect, qualifications were necessary to acquire work, but that school had not

alerted them to the link between qualifications and the labor market. The findings of this research diverge from Willis' analysis also in that, as described in the preceding chapter, the labor market could channel the young people into "part-time" or temporary low-paid work because of the financial vulnerability of the young people and their family. It was not from a confidence in their labor market position that they left school early; leaving school early occurred because the labor market drew these young people into employment and this met short-term needs. The factory management then discarded the young people when a slump in the market occurred.

Applying resistance theory, then, to the findings of this research uncovers resistance on the part of the young people to the educational system; however, no evidence is found to support one of the fundamental contentions of resistance theory—that of a class penetration of the educational paradigm. The findings support to some extent the findings of Willis, and evidence emerges to support resistance theory as defined by Willis as forming part of the overall reproduction of the working class. The findings support resistance theory without quite proving a class consciousness of resistance, but on the basis that class conflict is the root of their resistance to the schooling systems. Important differences emerge that could be explained by the fact that this research is based on a slightly different population. Overall, the findings give evidence of resistance as a reaction to schooling on the part of the young people studied. However, this resistance is presented by the young people as being derived more from their suppression by the educational system than from a culture creatively producing a resistance in the way in which Willis suggests. The reaction of the young people to schooling can be extremely destructive as opposed to culturally creative.

6

Beyond
a Social Research Framework

This chapter focuses on portraying the value of a reproduction/
resistance analysis of early school-leaving while, at one and the
same time, arguing that it is necessary to move beyond this conceptual framework because of its theoretical and political limitations. The social research framework, within which these theories
are framed, does not offer us sufficient tools for the transformative
politics that the crisis of space of early school-leaving requires. It
is not my intention to reject completely the reproduction and resistance problematic, as it does provide invaluable insights into
class structural processes and cultural resistance. Rather, I wish to
present the value of this type of analysis so as to draw attention
later to its theoretical miscalculations and limitations, combined
with its political weaknesses. This chapter attempts to acknowledge in detail the best of the reproductionist/resistance point of
view on early school-leaving, so that its insights and limitations
are seen in a specific analysis that will allow us to begin to go
beyond, while building on, the social research framework.

The reproduction/resistance reading of the previous chapter
provides us with a valuable understanding of the school-leaver's

social situation vis-à-vis class relations, as I now outline in this chapter.

EDUCATIONAL UNDERACHIEVEMENT

Young people from lower socioeconomic backgrounds underachieve in school because they resist schooling. They resist schooling on the basis of what they regard as the lack of relevance of the curriculum to their own socioeconomic background. This invariably leads to a situation of conflict between the pupils and the representatives of the schooling system. Paradoxically, the methods through which they resist underpins their educational underachievement.

They resist schooling in both a nonconflictual and a conflictual manner. On a nonconflictual level, they resist through nonparticipation or minimal participation and early school-leaving. They resist schooling in an open, conflictual manner by engaging in oppositional behavior directed against teachers or against school property. Oppositional behavior can operate at an indirect level that limits the demands made by the schooling system on the young people. Usually, however, oppositional behavior takes the form of direct opposition to the teachers' authority. In fact some oppositional behavior, due partially to group dynamics and partially to the depth of class antagonism, becomes extremely aggressive and destructive. Early school-leavers place themselves in opposition to the schooling system and its representatives. Hence, while this state of conflict exists, there is no possibility of an educational process occurring. In brief, the young people underachieve by rejecting the schooling system and the schooling authorities.

Culturally, their resistance is visible and has actually developed a cultural language: for example, "Doing a bunk." Not only this, their cultural support enables the young people to resist the individualization of failure that is embedded in the philosophy of the meritocratic ideal of the educational system.

Analyzing the conversations from a reproduction/resistance perspective does convey structural trends that highlighted the educational system's part in determining educational underachieve-

ment and early school-leaving. The young people expressed their
resistance to schooling as a reaction to the following structural
impositions of the system that were intolerable to them:

1. They point out that the school curriculum did not have any relevance
   to manual labor. Their argument is supported by the fact that the
   formal educational system's curriculum has a low emphasis on
   manual labor.
2. The educational system did not educate the young people from
   lower socioeconomic backgrounds to recognize the link between
   high educational qualifications and high financial rewards. The
   schooling system has, therefore, failed to relate to the background of
   those being taught. This is indeed a strange oversight on the part of
   the schooling system, given that the basic principles of education are
   to discern potentialities inherent in the pupils themselves and to
   incorporate their background in their development. It is also surpris-
   ing to note that the system failed to point out the economic worth of
   qualifications, which could certainly have served as an inducement
   to those economically deprived to proceed with their schooling.

The young early school-leavers explain that their oppositional
behavior and nonparticipation was due in part to being allocated to
low-grade classes where no teaching whatsoever was in progress.
This is highlighted by the fact that when the young people leave
school, most of them have basic literacy and numeracy problems.
Another element of the schooling system identified by the young
people which played a part in bringing about their oppositional
behavior is a discriminatory element on the part of the schooling
authorities. They point out that the schooling authorities do not
identify with those from lower socioeconomic backgrounds. This
invariably leads to a situation of conflict. Indeed this conflict is
carried into the community. Parents are convinced that the schooling authorities discriminate against their children. This in turn
reinforces the cultural awareness that the school authorities act
unfairly toward them because of their socioeconomic background.
A final aspect of the schooling system that contributed to their
underachievement was a structural collusion between the schooling system and the young people's nonparticipation. When the
young people behave in an oppositional manner, the teachers react
by withdrawing their teaching skills. Since the young people will

not accept discipline, absenteeism is in the interest of both teache and schools. Thus, a structural reproduction pattern is evident. Th young people resist schooling in reaction to discriminatory facets of the schooling system which they can identify as militating against them, and in doing so they enable the reproduction of their class position. It can be concluded that these young people from lower socioeconomic backgrounds underachieve because they resist schooling, resistance here meaning an individual and group resentment of and reaction to class subordination. The resistance by the subjects in this research is directed not predominantly by a "momentary glimpse of freedom," but by anger against the terms of their social and economic conditions, conditions that are mirrored in the terms of their schooling. It is directed more by a reaction to structural constraints than by cultural creativity, even though the culture supports resistance to schooling. In fact, the word "creativity" does not reflect the mood of the resistance outlined here whatsoever. In sum, the theoretical concept of resistance in use here is, in a general sense, that used by Willis but refers to a resistance derived more from class conflict and cultural constraints than from cultural penetrations and cultural creativity.

EARLY SCHOOL-LEAVING

While they resist school and educationally underachieve, the young people recognize that it is simply not progressive for them to remain there. In their own terms they recognize that they are "getting nowhere." Hence, they realize that if they are to experience any social or economic development in any small measure, it can only be achieved outside their schooling experience.

Three factors are involved in their early school-leaving. First, they want to leave school early. When they leave school they consider they have achieved freedom from a suppressive system. Even when they are unable to find employment, they are still convinced they have achieved a freedom that they will not relinquish. There is no "going back" to school. Second, by engaging in oppositional behavior the young people have made themselves vulnerable to the retaliatory or disciplinary sanctions of the system. They are expelled from school. Finally, it is an acceptable experience of the lower socioeconomic culture to leave school early. In lower socioeconomic communities there is no undesirable definition of early school-leaving. They simply cannot culturally integrate an undesirable definition, since the schooling system appears to militate against their cultural background.

ACCEPTANCE OF LABOR MARKET POSITION

Once the young people resist schooling, the overall economic system manages to play a more direct role of reproduction by offering a labor-market position that is an alternative to schooling, but one that contains little financial reward. Since the economic system offers the possibility of obtaining employment, albeit low-paid, this exercises a dual pressure on people from lower socioeconomic backgrounds to leave school early and to take up their position on the labor force. The labor market has a need for a part-time temporary labor force. This type of work attracts young people from a lower socioeconomic background since it is the only alternative to schooling. There is a conditioning to these terms of employment already operative in their socioeconomic background. A second pressure ensues from the economic system. Pressure is put on the young person to obtain an income because parents cannot afford financially to maintain their children at school. Furthermore, indirect pressure is put on the children to leave school and find employment. The young people themselves have not had access to finances and usually their families are living either on subsistence money from the state or on a low income.

It can be read that young people from lower socioeconomic backgrounds resist school because of the suppressive nature of the schooling system and schooling authorities. They opt for leaving school early due to their resistance, and this resistance is culturally supported. This can be seen by the fact that there is no negative social definition of early school-leaving held by those from this background. Having rejected schooling without having achieved any educational qualifications, they have no choice but to accept low-paid work and/or unemployment.

Their resistance to schooling, according to early school-leavers, is forced by the schooling system's manipulation of events such as its irrelevant curriculum and its discriminatory attitude toward the young people themselves. Their early school-leaving and acceptance of low-paid work is forced on them by their wish to escape from the social suppression of schooling and from the low financial income of their families.

A POSTSTRUCTURALIST PERSPECTIVE

The analysis above represents a structuralist/culturalist attempt to deal with the issue of early school-leaving through a reproductionist and resistance problematic. The arguments are represented forcefully, and so the reader at this point is probably more focused on the insights afforded than on the limitations of the conceptual framework. However, while recognizing the value of the insights afforded, I will now argue that it is necessary to move beyond this type of analysis. Inherent in it is a prevailing logic that shows *how it is* and gives us an understanding of *why it is* the way it is. Yet there is no theorizing of how it should be or could be, and so our understanding is allowed to fall into a political vacuum where the constructed "logic" ties the issue in a bind, rather than untying it. As can be seen from the above, once "the" structural story is told we have conclusions but no solutions. To enable solutions we need to begin to untell the master story, to unwind the reading that binds. It is no longer possible to maintain this theoretical framework totally since it is steeped in the "objectivism," determinacy, and notion of working-class centrality as elaborated by classical Marxism. A poststructuralist perspective can deconstruct some of these academic and theoretical constructions of the space of early school-leavers that, despite the best of intentions, often act as scaffolding to the material problems being lived by the early school-leavers themselves. The first move in a poststructuralist perspective is the questioning or deconstruction of the above analysis. This can be approached, first, through a historicization of the constructed logic of the reproduction/resistance analysis.

Very striking in this analysis is its presentation of the indomitable force of the reproductive system. Not only is there no escape for the young people, but the above framework does not even appear to be looking for one. It is as if, by describing and describing again how bad the situation is, it will miraculously change. If the text points out how bad the situation is, if it describes it continually, will this automatically lead to change? Certainly not. Absent from this is any notion of the pedagogical dimension to change or the necessity of theorizing strategies for change. In this sense the most serious weakness of reproduction/resistance analysis is clearly evident here. The belief in the power of domination held by the reproductive forces binds the mind of the theorist. The problem is left posed, but it dangles unresolved. A deconstruction of the conceptualization of the problem is not even attempted, nor is the human, social, and political responsibility of transformation in relation to early school-leavers ever assumed.

The resistance approach only goes so far as to present the underside of reproduction theory. The reliance of resistance theory on reproduction theory leaves them almost as one. Resistance theory as applied in this analysis in no way escapes the structural determinism of the reproductionist analysis, in fact it actually furthers it. Yet resistance theory came to fruition in order to escape determinism and argue for a more voluntarist approach. Resistance theory appears trapped in a binary relation to reproduction theory, and as such—even as it tries to force the debate into a transformative arena—it falls short because of this dependence.

A further weakness of this text, derived from its reliance on reproduction/resistance theory with its theoretical limitations, is apparent in the treatment of the gender issue. Reproduction/resistance analysis, Marxist in origin, gives centrality to the working class as the only agent of social change. The classist emphasis of these analyses is overwhelming. Race and gender relations of oppression are not taken into consideration or theorized within the analysis. While, in the specific context of the conversations, race is not a factor in the oppression, gender most certainly is. The class-reduction emphasis of these theories produces an illusion that the gender issue is being dealt with just because it includes young women in its remit. While class is extremely important to the analysis of early school-leaving, this limitation of reproduction/resistance theory leaves a situation where the gendering that occurs cannot be taken up theoretically. The analysis, consequently, does not examine this form of suppression or how gendering affects young boys' and girls' early school-leaving differently. It leaves unexamined the coming together of the two moments of oppression—gendering and early school-leaving—and their relation to each other. The analysis is essentially blind to the part gendering plays in shaping early school-leaving, despite the fact that direct references are made to this by the early school-leavers in the dialogues.

The issue of cultural production as a potentially powerful and potentially emancipatory force is ignored in this text. If the analysis had stayed strictly within the parameters of reproduction theory, it would have been obvious that the young people were being allowed no voice and had no agency. However, in incorporating the insights of a resistance approach, they are given room for voice, and to a certain extent an agency, but ironically this is used only to prove that they have no power in their voice, nor agency over their lives. Power is seen as a dominating force, not as a productive force. This view runs squarely counter to that of Foucault, who has argued persuasively in a number of texts against this "negative" view of power, as argued by the repressive hypothesis. Against this conception, Foucault advances the thesis of a great diversity and versatility of power relations. In particular, Foucault argues that: "We must cease once and for all to describe the effects of power in negative terms: it 'excludes,' it 'represses,' it 'censors,' it 'abstracts,' it 'masks,' it 'conceals.' In fact power produces reality; it produces domains of objects and rituals of truth" (1980, p. 194). For Foucault power relations are not some invisible hand programming social reality; rather they are in constant flux and are eminently transformable. Power may be omnipresent, but it is also omni-changeable. So, in conclusion, while resistance theory appears more politically aware because it gives voice to the excluded, this voice is not given power and agency insofar as the struggle for a political space for early school-leavers is neglected.

If resistance theory were not so bound to reproductive explanations, and if social research were more committed to the politics of transformative theorizing, the analysis could have gone another way. Since there is ample evidence of resistance by early school-leavers, and of political understandings on their part, an attempt could have been made to theorize how this could be politically, culturally, and pedagogically engaged so as to feed into emancipatory strategies. Hence the necessity to make a paradigm shift from the class-based structuralist discourse to a poststructuralist language and perspective. Chapter 7 attempts to do this by engaging

the issue of early school-leaving, the material space of early
school-leavers, and the discursive construction of the space of
early school-leavers from the point of view of transformative theorizing. From this vantage point, a cultural and pedagogical politics
of early school-leaving is theorized in Chapter 8, which uses the
insights afforded by reproduction and resistance theory while also
seeking to redress the political limitations of these problematics.

This book is about contributing to a post–reproduction/resis-
tance theory and politics, Part III providing the *post*–reproduction/
resistance dimension in terms of transformative theories and a cultural politics. Chapter 7 will engage the reproduction/resistance
theoretical analysis presented here, in that it deconstructs Marxism
as a master narrative and shows the theoretical limitations of some
of its concepts including reproduction/resistance theory.

NEW POLITICAL SPACES—
A PROJECT AND PRACTICE?

Part II introduced the notion that early school-leavers represent a political crisis of space which has two dimensions.[1] First, there is the political crisis of the specific material space of early school-leavers—they have demands, they engage in concrete resistances, and they struggle for a sphere of influence around which they can construct empowering identities. The second aspect of the crisis can be described as discursive. There is an absence of a discursive political formation that would articulate the relations of subordination as relations of oppression and domination which could act as an external referent against which the specifics of a political location for early school-leavers can be formulated.

This section conceptualizes early school-leaving in terms of a political crisis of space, as opposed to simply defining early school-leaving as a "problem" for strategic reasons. First, the struggle of early school-leavers can be defined as a political struggle. Second, this political problematic will allow me to name their struggle for education, work, respect, and equality as a democratic struggle. Third, as argued by Jameson (in Stephanson, 1988, pp. 3–21) the notion of space creates an image of a certain fluidity in social and cultural processes which will facilitate the intellectual imagining and construction of new conditions.

The theoretical benefit of using the concepts of "political crisis of space" and "new political spaces" is that these terms suggest a shift from a modernist or Marxist narrative to a new language that could represent and express an open-ended terrain of political possibilities. It is possible that at this stage we need new ways of

125

conceiving the social, in order to deconstruct old and reconstruct new sets of historical possibilities. This means constructing a new language, as Ernesto Laclau puts it: "a new language means, as you know, new objects, new problems, new values, and the possibility of discursively constructing new antagonisms and forms of struggle" (Laclau, 1991, p. 162).

New languages and new theories are needed to understand the specific space opened up by the issue of early school-leaving. The struggle of early school-leavers is constituted within the ensemble of practices and discourses that create the different forms of subordination they experience. Important here is the idea that to theorize a new political space for early school-leavers involves an understanding of the concept of space as a discursive construction. Arising from this awareness, the historicity of the current construction of early school-leaving can be seen and the practical and discursive dimension to this crisis can be recognized. Thus, a new discursive space that articulates a politics for early school-leavers becomes appropriate.

The previous chapters have argued that the redressing of this crisis of early school-leaving needs to be taken up as a political imperative. Part III attempts to play a part in this by giving priority to the political interpretation of early school-leaving; by identifying early school-leaving as signifying a political crisis of location; by naming their everyday resistances and cultural production of meanings as constituting a political struggle; and by creating a new political terrain of struggle through conceptualizing and articulating a specific cultural politics of early school-leaving.

NOTE

1. This formulation of a dual political crisis of space of early school-leaving is largely derived from the concept as formulated by Fredric Jameson: see A. Stephanson, "Regarding Postmodernism: A Conversation with Fredric Jameson," in *Universal Abandon?*, edited by Andrew Ross (Minneapolis, MN: University of Minnesota Press, 1988, pp. 3–31)

7

Transformative Theories

The only theory that is worth having is that which you have to fight off, not that which you speak with profound fluency.

Stuart Hall, cited in Grossberg, Nelson, & Treichler, 1992

The previous chapters should leave the reader with a sense of the material struggle of the early school-leavers. It is made clear through their dialogue that the lack of income, employment, and social status are serious problems for these young people and that they live out their lives struggling to improve their situation. We know that there is a problem, that there is a struggle, but is there a political practice to advance this struggle? This chapter illustrates how new theoretical developments might create the terrain for a cultural and pedagogical politics of early school-leaving.

Tackling the issue of early school-leaving in the 1990s involves diverse political and cultural strategies that can be located within the realm of a poststructuralist theory of the discursive construction of power relations and dynamics. This theoretical perspective forges links between the site-based discourse and practice of early school-leavers as described and constructed in Part I, and broader discourses that will be introduced here.

The decade of the 1990s sees us in a different theoretical and political arena from that of the 1960s and 1970s. The last three decades have seen the development of a poststructuralist/post-modern debate in social theory on new theoretical and social movements that are bringing each other to crisis. For example, postcolonial movements have brought master narratives of the West to a crisis point. Therefore, a modernist Marxist narrative is critiqued for its economism, for its meta-narrative status, and for being steeped in Western ideology with its inherent notions of exclusion. A modernist feminist narrative is now seen to have told only one story, namely a Eurocentric one. Feminism and feminist theory, on the other hand, may have brought about the breakdown of the paternal metaphor, a breakdown that affects both master narratives of the West and postcolonial articulations. These theoretical and social developments, even if expressed in terms of "crisis," have not undermined the urgency of the political, but they have left us in a position where we have to theorize how to proceed with the politics of social change.

Part II offered a Marxist analysis of the problem of early school-leaving and an attempt to move beyond it. Of direct relevance to this project is the current poststructuralist contention that Marxism as a master narrative is in crisis and thus the entire socialist project is in disarray. Laclau and Mouffe are specific on this issue:

> What is now in crisis is a whole conception of socialism which rests upon the ontological centrality of the working class, upon the role of Revolution, with a capital "r," as the founding moment in the transition from one type of society to another, and upon the illusory prospects of a perfectly unitary and homogeneous collective will that will render pointless the moment of politics. The plural and multifarious character of contemporary social struggles has finally dissolved the last foundation for that political imaginary. [Laclau & Mouffe, 1985, p. 2]

The struggle of the early school-leavers can in this spirit be said to be of a "plural" and "multifarious" character, with no guarantees that their struggle will be progressive or revolutionary, nor even conceptualized or articulated as a struggle. We know that early school-leavers exist in a material and discursive location of subordination, but the problem is multidimensional and cannot automatically be solved through any Marxist "Revolution." So where do we go from here?

In order to proceed we could begin to engage the struggle of early school-leavers on a transformative theoretical level. Up to this point, this book has simply named and described a politicized account of the existing construction of the social reality of early school-leaving. The practical and discursive dimension of the exclusion of early school-leavers has been explored, and they have, in their dialogue, given expression to the everyday aspects of their struggle. Now, however, it is important to take up a more transformative role in the struggle—to contribute to the creation of a new political space for early school-leavers. This involves articulating their struggle in a new way. In order to do this I will first move away from the "objective" language of critique and description and move into a political language of transformation and possibility.

This chapter engages two new theoretical paradigms—post-Marxism and cultural studies. From these, it abstracts two theoretical frameworks—radical social democracy and cultural production—and applies them to the issue of early school-leaving. I use these in order to propel the project of early school-leavers forward, toward emancipatory and radically democratic goals. I argue that these theories of radical social democracy and theories of cultural production provide a transformative theoretical framework from which the issue of early school-leaving can be moved discursively beyond its current political crisis of space. These transformative theories suggest that the struggle of early school-leavers can be articulated as a new, forceful, and emancipatory struggle.

RADICAL SOCIAL DEMOCRACY
AND EARLY SCHOOL-LEAVERS

Poststructuralist theoretical developments can be seen to open up new possibilities for transformation. While various new theoretical and social movements are bringing each other to crisis, there is a new intellectual movement on the "left" which is interested in rewriting this crisis as productive for a political re-theorizing of radical social change.

This text is situated within the emergent discourse of "radical" or "empowered" democracy. In the last decade, a number of writers from different positions have sought to go beyond the Marxist modernist vision of democracy to articulate a more positive counter to the restricted vision of liberal democratic theorists. The influential Italian political philosopher Norberto Bobbio began in the mid-1970s to posit a "revisionist" view of the relationship between Marxism, socialism, and democracy (1976). Reflecting the abiding influence of Antonio Gramsci on Italian political thinking, Bobbio called for a revalorization of civil society and argued that the future of socialism is tied ineluctably to the future of democracy. These themes were reflected in the United States through, among others, the work of Stanley Aronowitz on the role of culture in Marxist theory (1981). Henry Giroux, for his part, sought to focus on how cultural workers could deepen the meaning of radical democracy through a postmodern practice that would emphasize the politics of difference (1992).

Roberto Mangabeira Unger seeks a broad transformation of the social sciences and their relationship with the struggle to transform social life. In his three-volume work entitled *Politics, A Work in Constructive Social Theory*, he devotes considerable space to detail a program of "empowered democracy" (1987). This radical project challenges traditional modes of understanding the world which fail to recognize the inherent plasticity of society and thus the possibilities for transformation. For early school-leavers, locked into a situation that they and others perceive as both structural and "natural," the liberatory potential of this viewpoint is obvious. Following Unger's critique of the social sciences, we can see how much educational studies have succumbed to a view of what Unger terms "false necessity." In failing to grasp the mutability of contexts, and in accepting that the outcome of social struggles is determined by forces we cannot alter, most social thinkers have bid farewell to any radical project of transformation. According to Unger, we can now reject the idea that society has a natural order and the vice of false necessity (things must be as they are). While the precise details of Ungers's vision of an empowered democracy may need to be "operationalized," as an alternative to the current crisis of transformation strategies it must be attractive.

Though all these writings on radical democracy are pertinent to the project of building transformative theory, I will concentrate on the work of Ernesto Laclau and Chantal Mouffe who attempt a bold construction of a new political discourse. Though they are widely criticized by more orthodox Marxists,[1] I wish to concentrate on the transformative tools they develop to engage the issue of early school-leaving in such a way as to bring the struggle of early school-leavers into a new political space. Their struggle could thus be articulated within a project of radical democracy. I briefly outline here the Laclau–Mouffe project for constructing a radical democracy, and then relate this discourse to the political struggle of early school-leavers. I use the categories developed by Laclau and Mouffe, but when applied to this specific issue they do become somewhat modified.

Laclau and Mouffe write from a post-Marxist position, transforming and critiquing the Marxist problematic in their belief that it has inherent discursive limitations in relation to comprehending contemporary social relations. However, rather than dismissing the Marxist theoretical and political project, they historicize it. They situate it within the broader democratic revolution of the present era, excavating it for strategic insights that can still speak toward the struggle for equality and liberty. In their deconstruction of Marxism, they call upon poststructuralist insights and a particular postmodern conception of politics. They also critique Marxism from a concrete political terrain, namely the practical developments in radical politics since the 1960s. They believe that Marxism as a totalizing narrative is unable to theorize the growing fragmentation associated with late capitalism or the new forms of antagonism that prevail toward the end of the twentieth century. They argue that there has been an increase in democratic public spaces evident from the proliferation of new identities and new antagonisms, associated with the rise of the "new" social movements such as feminism, gay and lesbian rights, and nuclear disarmament and ecology movements. The increasing fragmentation of social classes has led to a rapid politicization of social relations and increasingly labile political identities. Laclau and Mouffe attempt to conceptualize the possibilities that inhere in these existing political struggles. They provide the conceptual framework and tools to engage and critique Marxism, to theorize contemporary concrete political practices, and to reformulate, or construct, a radical democratic politics.

Laclau and Mouffe break with the traditional nineteenth-century conceptualization of the social. In their work they argue that the main discursive limitation characteristic of nineteenth-century social theory, including Marxism, is an "objectivism" in the comprehension of social relations. By objectivism Laclau means "the assumption that society may be understood as an objective and coherent ensemble from foundations or laws of movement that are conceptually graspable" (Strategies Collective, 1988, p. 13). If something is seen as objective, its being is considered to be both fully present and always preconstituted. There is a "being" of history and society that constitutes their ultimate reality and needs only to be uncovered. The progress of knowledge and the development of a discipline amounts to the discovery of layers of objective laws. Laclau and Mouffe reject "objectivism" for theoretical and political reasons, because concepts such as "antagonisms," "negativity," "struggle," and "revolutionary action" cannot fit comfortably into this understanding of the social.

In contrast to this "objectivism," Laclau and Mouffe advance a more fluid and active perspective on society and social relations. They assert the ultimate impossibility of all "objectivity" (Strategies Collective, 1988, p. 15):

> Against this, the perspective we hold affirms the *constitutive* and *primordial* character of negativity. All social order, as a consequence, can only affirm itself insofar as it represses a " constitutive outside" which negates it—which amounts to saying that social order never succeeds in entirely constituting itself as an objective order. It is in that sense that we have sustained the *revelatory* character of antagonism: what is shown in antagonism is the *ultimate* impossibility of social objectivity. [Strategies Collective, 1988, p. 13]

"Objectivity" fails because society can be seen to be constituted through divergent antagonistic forces, and not through a unifying logic. A radical contingency is apparent in society, and the "objectivity" of the social can be seen to be simply a historical construction. Laclau and Mouffe argue that the radical contingency of the social shows itself in the experience of these social antagonisms. Within this framework, the world is seen less as a "given" and more as a radical social construction. Social structures are not totally closed but, rather, are dislocated. These social antagonisms dislocate or decenter the social structure. They argue that these "structural dislocations" and the radical contingency of these structural dislocations that stem from the pressure of antagonistic forces arguably create the basis for a new set of possibilities for historical action.

In classical Marxism there was a concentration on the social maladjustments and dislocations generated by capitalism, with these dislocations being seen as having an objective meaning that could be incorporated within a Marxist narrative. According to this problematic, the subject of change is internal to, and absorbed by, the structure. In a post-Marxist perspective the "location" of the subject is that of dislocation. In classical Marxism, social change was theorized through the simplification of the social structure and the privileging of one agent of social change—the working class. On the other hand, in a post-Marxist perspective, historical possibilities are opened up due to a proliferation of new subjects of change that arise from the dislocations associated with contemporary capitalism. Laclau and Mouffe argue that contemporary capitalism tends to multiply these points of dislocation, creating a plurality of new antagonisms, which in turn are linked to the multiplication of the subjects of change. The intrinsic negativity of all antagonism does not allow us to fix on the "objectivity" of any one social agent, such as the working class. Rather, within this perspective, social agents are seen as radically contingent and open to new reformulations.[2]

To assure the reader that this trajectory is worth investigating, let me briefly relate these notions of "the failure of objectivity," "structural dislocations," "radical contingency," and "new possibilities for historical action" to the issue of early school-leaving. I would argue that these concepts give us a framework to rethink the issue of early school-leaving. In relating the understanding of "the ultimate impossibility of all objectivity" to an understanding of early school-leaving, the "objectivism" of reproduction and resistance theories becomes visible. In reproduction theory, relations of reproduction are visualized as being objective because they are conceptualized as present and fully constituted. However, according to a post-Marxist reading, these relations are not seen to exist objectively, because this "objectivity" is viewed as a social construction. This asserts not that reproduction fails to take place but, rather, the radical historicity and ultimate arbitrariness and incompleteness of reproduction as a process. What now emerges is that the reproduction of early school-leavers is associated with divergent forces and that the outcome of this process is not decided by any "objective" law in advance but, rather, is found to be arbitrary, incomplete, and radically contingent.

The radical contingency of the reproductive forces at work displays itself in the experience of antagonism. In the case of early school-leaving, the antagonism is clearly evident between the early school-leavers and the school and its representatives. Reproduction takes place through a struggle, the outcome of which is not dictated in advance. The early school-leavers are antagonized, they resist, and this resistance can be seen as the "constitutive outside," the moment of failure of "objectivity".

Resistance theory is also influenced by "objectivism," though to a lesser extent than is reproduction theory. Because resistance theory operates in binary opposition to reproduction theory, it gears itself toward showing the voluntary side of determinate social relations associated with the process of schooling. In a sense it reinforces the sedimentation of the "objectivity" of the forces of reproduction, because it does not contest the arbitrariness and historicity associated with all forms of theorizing. The resistance of early school-leavers is not seen as an antagonism that decenters reproductive relations, nor as evidence of a structural dislocation. Rather, resistance of "working-class kids" or of early school-leavers is simply seen to feed back into the determinate and unavoidable relations of reproduction. Reproduction theory traditionally gives overwhelming authority to the structural dimension of the reproduction of class relations, while resistance theory in turn gives added authority to the individual's role in the reproduction of the capitalist order. Both theories place the early school-leaver in a position of being structurally determined in that they are seen to act according to certain structural determinants.

The reproduction/resistance analysis of Chapter 5 is clearly influenced by the "objectivism" of the reproduction/resistance framework. Early school-leavers' resistance is explored because they are looked on as the privileged agents of social change, being predominantly from working-class backgrounds and visibly resisting relations of subordination. However, from a traditional Marxist point of view, there is a disappointing aspect to this resistance— the supposed agents do not achieve the revolutionary change expected of them. The analysis accepts that a capitalist dislocation with respect to early school-leaving occurs, but it is concluded that the subjects of possible revolutionary change—early school-leavers—are absorbed by the structure.

A different interpretation of the resistance we found in early school-leavers is possible if we develop a post-Marxist problematic. According to a post-Marxist understanding, there are multiple dislocations associated with contemporary society. This is seen to lead to a plurality of antagonisms, with the location of the subject of this change being part of that dislocation. Within this perspective, early school-leaving and early school-leavers' resistance signifies one of many dislocations generated by capitalism. The radical contingency of the social shows itself in this antagonism and resistance by the early school-leaver. The early school-leavers' resistance does not signify a moment of reproduction but, rather, is the result of the failure of this structure of reproduction. The arbitrariness of reproduction is apparent at this point of dislocation, and it is at this very point that the movement of its affirmation is radically contingent. Whether, in practice, the resistance of early school-leavers feeds back into the reproductive system or whether we construct this resistance in terms of agency is to a certain extent arbitrary, historical, and dependent on articulation. This is a crucial insight with respect to building strategies of a cultural politics of early school-leavers. It discloses that resistance can be strategically articulated in new, more emancipatory ways.

A post-Marxist construction of radical democracy begins from the general point of asserting the "arbitrariness of the social." If the social is arbitrary, then a socialist *strategy* is both necessary and worthwhile. For Laclau, a hegemonic socialist strategy involves:

> the contingent articulation of elements around certain social con-
> figurations—historical blocs—that cannot be predetermined by
> any philosophy of history and that is essentially linked to the
> concrete struggles of social agents. By *concrete* I mean *specific*,
> in all their humble individuality and materiality, not insofar as
> they incarnate the dream of intellectuals about a "universal
> class." [Strategies Collective, 1988, p. 16]

Laclau and Mouffe have begun to theorize new possibilities for radical democratic change. They believe that possibilities arise in the context of the structural dislocations evidenced by new social movements. They not only theorize the construction of the social, but "of social agents who transform themselves and forge new identities as a result" (Laclau, 1991, p. 40). How do they envisage the construction of these new social agents that are intrinsic to a radical democracy? Can this theory be applied to the construction of early school-leavers as social agents? Can this discourse of radical democracy act as a referent for the political struggle of early school-leavers?

In post-Marxist theory, subjects of change exist because of dis-locations in the social structures. There is a source of freedom in the event of structural dislocation, because where structural faults arise the construction of social identity can only take place through acts of identification. An act of identification arising from a struc-tural dislocation is both an act of power and a radically contingent act. This, in effect, opens up a certain fluidity around the construc-tion of any social identity. Within this perspective the acts of iden-tification can go in different directions—the direction depends on how the identity is articulated.

Laclau and Mouffe argue that contemporary late capitalism multiplies the structural dislocations experienced in our society. This multiplication is linked to the fragmentation and growing limitation of social actors. A situation arises wherein more areas of social life must become the product of political forms of recon-struction and regulation. The conceptualization of new spaces and social imaginaries which will transform these dislocations into radically democratic political demands becomes central. Because of the fragmentation associated with contemporary capitalism social issues become the rallying point for various social struggles. The articulation of the demands that arise from the concentration on social issues gathers strength to challenge the political system with growing demands for justice and equality. However, because of fragmentation, social issues acquire a certain autonomy in relation to social structures. This means that the indeterminacy of the social relations between the different demands of social actors opens the possibility of the articulation of these demands by either the left or the right political discourses. The development of a socialist democratic imaginary, within which the articulations of these demands are organized, is crucial to ensuring the expansion of these struggles as radically democratic struggles. If this is not in place the demands can begin, and do begin, to be articulated under a fascist or racist umbrella. For example, "give us a job" becomes "keep foreigners out."

Laclau and Mouffe address themselves toward the problem of identifying the discursive conditions necessary for the emergence of collective action which would direct its energies toward struggling against inequalities and challenging relations of subordination. They develop and expand the Gramscian concept of hegemony as a logic of the social that provides an "anchorage from which contemporary social struggles are thinkable in their specificity" (Laclau & Mouffe, 1985). In other words, they develop a politics that does not do a disservice to social struggles such as those of the early school-leavers, feminism, and ecological or working-class struggles, but one that leaves their specificity intact. They argue that what allows forces of resistance to assume the character of collective struggles is the existence of an external discourse of radical democracy that "impedes the stabilization of subordination as difference" (Laclau & Mouffe, 1985, p. 159). In this context, a new social movement could retain its specificity but might politically support other social movements on particular issues in an overall effort to struggle effectively and collectively for the ideals of justice and equality.

Given Laclau and Mouffe's theoretical and political framework, the question I must now ask is, in what ways does it speak to the issue of early school-leaving? Do early school-leavers represent a crisis of space or, in the words of Laclau and Mouffe, a structural dislocation? An antagonism emerges within the educational system which decenters the social structure resulting in the need for an act of identification on the part of early school-leavers. A struggle over identification takes place. On the one hand, there are those powerful educational discourses that construct the early school-leaver as "not bright," "underachiever," "troublemaker," as having "no sticking power," as coming from "disturbed family relations," or as being "culturally deprived." A subordinate identity is constructed for early school-leavers by these discourses which attempts to deprive them of naming the present social relations as relations of oppression. This then prevents them from naming their everyday struggle against these relations of oppression as being political. Though their subject position is constructed in relations of subordination, do early school-leavers choose or adopt any of these negative identities?

While these subordinating educational discourses are privileged and acquire strength from the asymmetrical relations that support them, they are certainly not all-powerful. While it is true that early school-leavers occupy *a* subordinated subject position that diminishes the power of their voice and delegitimates their everyday experiences and knowledge, this does not constitute the total story. A struggle over identification does take place. Because they occupy multiple subject positions, some of them more emancipatory than others, they can draw on these to resist their subordination as early school-leavers. For example, they could draw on their subject position as workers to demand a fair wage, or they could draw on their subject position as Irish citizens to demand equal treatment. Early school-leavers can, and do, contest and reject the negative identity construction that is articulated for them by the dominant educational discourses. Their subject position as early school-leaver does not totally deny them the right to speak. Their experiences can never be entirely delegitimated, and sometimes they can be articulated in publicly legitimate ways. Even the most calculated and powerful attempt to deny the entitlement of speech to early school-leavers cannot be totally effective since early school-leavers retain an ability to articulate individual and communal forms of resistance.

Breaking down the negative identity of early school-leavers is possible, and this book is part of just such a process. First, the recorded conversations illustrate how, and in what ways, a specific group of early school-leavers do engage in alternative articulations of their schooling experience, giving full voice to the various forms of injustice they have encountered. Their dialogue suggests that they do engage in their own acts of identification. Second, this text records their experiences, voices, and alternative discourses, bringing alternative articulations into a socially "legitimate" arena. Thirdly, in politicizing academic discourses we can begin to delegitimate the authoritative voice of the academy when it constructs a negative identity for the young early school-leaver.

The availability of an alternative discursive formation that could offer a space to articulate school-leavers' identity in a new way is strategically important to the early school-leavers' struggle for a positive identification. The struggle for a more empowering and explicitly political identification for early school-leavers could be aided strategically through the construction of a more egalitarian discursive formation. Laclau and Mouffe's theory of radical democracy can be used to articulate a new identity of democratic citizens with rights to educational qualifications, to a better income, and to a better way of life. This discourse supplies a social imaginary from which to name the social relations that give rise to early school-leaving as unjust. Furthermore, within this imaginary, early school-leavers can be theorized as potential social agents of radical democracy, since to challenge the relations surrounding their subordination and to articulate them as oppressive in effect deepens democracy by opening up a new critical public social sphere. A social agent of change can be an individual or a group that can accomplish specific activities through economic and political struggle. Early school-leavers *can* become social agents. What is necessary is a strategy that will transform the forms of identification and subjectivity that currently exist into new forms of identity linked to an agency that will be in tune with a conception of a radical social democracy. Laclau and Mouffe's discourse of radical democracy provides the necessary language of possibility from which to begin.

In conclusion, the discourse of radical democracy not only articulates the relations of early school-leaving as unjust, but also provides a further referent for the political struggle to create new material and discursive spaces. Though early school-leavers do not constitute a social movement as such, they do engage in forms of social struggle. Laclau and Mouffe theorize a politics that allows the specificity of the struggle of early school-leavers to be left intact. Yet, in engaging the struggle in terms of constructing a radical democracy, another political opportunity is created.

Using the theoretical and ethical referent of radical social democracy we can reinvent early school-leavers, not as victims, but as human agents with the democratic right to self- and social determination, to self- and social governance, and to a critical democratic public sphere of political struggle. Theoretically, the engagement of the issue of early school-leaving with the discourse of radical democracy helps to constitute a new space in which early school-leavers become the signifiers of a political crisis, and the signifiers of whether we have a failed or a successful democracy. It opens a theoretical discursive space in which they can become political activists and human agents insofar as they are educated toward empowerment and governance.

EARLY SCHOOL-LEAVERS
AND CULTURAL PRODUCTION

The notion of cultural production is theorized within a cultural studies paradigm. Cultural studies can be considered as an intellectual movement, a movement that continually negotiates theory in an inter-disciplinary or anti-disciplinary way toward achieving the ends of producing a politics of change. Its practitioners, by all accounts, see themselves as intervening in social change as politically engaged participants (see Grossberg et al., 1992). It is not quite possible to define cultural studies as a school of thought, though this has indeed been attempted.[3] The most recent and sensible attempt to synopsize "cultural studies" emerges from the 1991 international conference, "Cultural Studies Now and in the Future," held at the University of Illinois at Urbana–Champaign. Tony Bennett describes it as "largely a convenient label for a whole range of approaches which, however divergent they may be in other respects, share a commitment to examining cultural practices from the point of view of their intrication with, and within, relations of power" (in Grossberg et al., 1992, p. 33). He goes on to argue that these cultural studies approaches are only of worth insofar as they can be of service to practical engagements with, and within, the relations between culture and power.

In this chapter I focus on a central theoretical and political insight of the cultural studies paradigm—the specific value of a politics of cultural production. A politics of cultural production is of crucial importance to the development of new material and discursive spaces for early school-leavers. Indeed, it is important to the project of social reconstruction in general. First, the value of a politics of cultural production is that it can make a concrete contribution to local and specific strategies that transform the forms of identification and constructions of subjectivity that currently exist for early school-leavers into forms of identity with agency that are in keeping with the construction of a radical democracy. Second, a politics of cultural production extends the domain of politics in a direction that will not be strategically dominated by the forces of economic and social control. Third, acknowledging cultural production increases our understanding of social reality as a fluid process of construction. This understanding points to the possibility of a political strategy of cultural production and intervention.

An understanding of cultural production is needed as a strategic tool for transformative politics. More specifically, it is needed to theorize the reconstruction of the material and political space of early school-leavers. This section proceeds by first outlining the theoretical development of a poststructuralist/post-Marxist concept of culture that conceives of culture as being centrally productive, as having the power to reshape social life, and as inhabiting materiality as opposed to being external to it. I will outline how this development offers us central strategic insights into the social reconstruction of society. This will be related to the specific struggle this book engages through showing how it paves the way for constructing a cultural politics and a cultural critical pedagogy of, and for, early school-leavers.

The past twenty years were marked by a contentious debate on differing conceptions of culture. This debate has stimulated an expanded understanding of the nature of culture and the political possibilities inherent in its varied use. Yet no one particular definition has won dominance in the debate. The debate centers around the issues of the relationship between culture and materiality, or culture and social structure, and on what type of power we can accord to culture. For the political purposes of this book, a politically enabling post-Marxist/poststructuralist concept of culture and cultural production is chosen, and I would like briefly to trace the development of this concept.

New social theory has contested the traditional liberal concept of culture as encompassing the arts, the media, symbolic relations, or a selection of texts and artifacts from selective traditions. Orthodox Marxism conceived of culture as belonging to the superstructure. Within this perspective the material world is external to, and determines, the human one. The dynamic force of history and society is explained in terms of historical materialism. Yet in the political project of Marxism, it is expected that culture would act to overcome the forces of materialism. This marks one of the many contradictions between the Marxist objectivist version of historical materialism and the Marxist humanist political project embodied in the class struggle. In the later Marxist works, such as that of the Italian communist political philosopher and leader Antonio Gramsci, there is a move toward an expanded version of the power embodied in culture. In the structuralist Marxism of the French philosopher Louis Althusser, culture is named as the arena within which the contradictions that arise within a capitalist society are dealt with. While Althusser does still divide society into the base (economic conditions) and the superstructure (the effects of the economic base, including culture), he also refines this model by insisting that culture is not merely a reflection of the economic base, but could produce its own effects. There is a rejection of the mechanistic determination inherent in some varieties of Marxism. Althusser compromises by opting for a notion of "overdetermination" which does allow for the "relative autonomy" of cultural forces. This broadens the Marxist position on culture in that it envisages it as a function of power, of being more than a simple outcome of the reproduction of social structures. Culture is now seen to play a role in generating social subjects and distributing subject positions.

However, the poststructuralist concept of culture would see the Althusserian theory of culture as limited, in that Althusser conceives of culture as reproducing power but not contesting it. A poststructuralist critique of the Althusserian theory of culture is explored by Michael Ryan:

> The possibility that seemingly ideological cultural artifacts might be sites of important political tensions or that their ideology might itself be symptomatic of incipient struggles or that they might be antidotes to threatening popular potentials is not granted within the althusserian framework. [1989, p. 11]

During the early 1970s there was a move toward Gramsci's conceptualization of hegemony because it appeared to allow for a more productive account of culture. Tony Bennett describes the shift in Gramsci from the classical notions of "class domination" to the struggle for hegemony.

> Where Gramsci departed from the earlier Marxist tradition was in arguing that the cultural and ideological relations between ruling and subordinate classes in capitalist societies consist less in the *domination* of the latter by the former than in the struggle for *hegemony*—that is, for moral, cultural, intellectual and, thereby, political leadership over the whole of the society—between the ruling class and, as the principal subordinate class, the working class. [Bennett, Mercer, & Wolacott, 1986, p. xiv]

Within this perspective domination is something that is won, not just delivered through the class struggle but through certain cultural processes. Political power is something that is negotiated and legitimated through cultural production. For Gramsci (1971), cultural leadership involves the production of consent since hegemony is sustained only through the winning of this consent. This implies that a vigorous struggle continually takes place in a cultural arena. Inherent in this implication is an expanded version of the cultural domain. This provides a theoretical and practical entry into cultural processes absent in classical Marxist theory. Gramsci argues that change is built into the system. He acknowledges some power on the part of the human agent by showing that while there is an overdetermining structure producing the individual, there are also a range of possibilities being produced. In his historical work, he also addresses the construction of cultural power in specific cases throughout history.

While in Gramscian theory the area of cultural production and cultural processes is opened up, it is still seen as severely limited by extra-cultural conditions. For Gramsci, popular culture can contest and resist the ruling or bourgeoisie culture, yet the ruling class—because of its economic strength—still dominates. In Gramscian theory, it is the ruling-class culture that dominates at the popular cultural level. Therefore, it can be argued that this concept contains serious limitations for interpreting culture as a political force and cultural production as a political tool (Ryan, 1989).

During the 1970s and 1980s the writings of Gramsci and Althusser formed the basis of an ongoing enquiry into the terrain of culture at the Centre for Contemporary Cultural Studies (CCCS) in Birmingham. During the 1970s, research there moved from the theoretical writings of Althusser toward those of Gramsci, and the Centre's definition of culture broke away from the narrow meaning of a selection of texts and artifacts to a broader definition. Their new definition dealt with social formations, cultural power, domination and regulation, resistance and struggle. The post-Marxist/ poststructuralist critique of the work of the CCCS, however, is that their focus in culture is overassociated with cultural resistance. A more productive understanding of the underlying cultural processes is thus lost. A poststructuralist critique of the CCCS perspective on culture is that, though within this viewpoint hegemony is never stable and is always negotiated through struggle, the primary agent of cultural activity is still understood to be that of the dominant class. Thus Ryan argues that:

> The dominant class exercises its hegemony through culture, and the subordinate class, sex, and race are placed in a secondary position in relation to that hegemony. All they can do is resist a more primary vector of domination, which is accorded a determining priority. [Ryan, 1989, p. 18]

A poststructuralist/post-Marxist approach to culture entails a less restricted notion of culture and cultural production. The boundary between materiality and culture is deconstructed. Materiality is not seen as a purely extra-cultural determinant which stands outside the human will. From a poststructuralist perspective, culture can no longer be considered simply as counterposed to materiality—rather, it must be seen to have a power of construction that extends into social materiality. Following Ryan:

> In the poststructuralist perspective, culture inhabits materiality as the forms of social life, from the family to the workday to our very psychological dispositions. The forms and representational patterns of culture are not simply added onto an already constituted substance of social existence. The supplement of cultural form is that without which no sociality could be possible; decultured sociality would be a diffusion of formless and boundless energy or matter. [Ryan, 1989, p. 12]

This poststructuralist account of culture dissolves the notion of materiality as extracultural or as belonging totally outside rhetoric and the powers of social construction. Furthermore, there is a different conception of power behind this theory of culture. Culture is seen to be always in process as a productive force and as such does not reside in any one specific cultural location. What constitutes culture, then, are contesting forces that hegemony attempts to contain. It is argued that there is no primary vector of domination. Hegemony is itself a form of resistance to the constant forces of cultural production. There is an interplay of forces in contestation, rather than a total determining power. Ryan argues in this respect that:

> Rather than being understood simply as an instrument of hegemony, cultural forms can be read as sites of political difference, where domination and resistance, the resistance to the positive power of the dispossessed that is domination and the counterpower, the threat of reversed domination, that is the potential force of the dispossessed, meet. [Ryan, 1989, p. 19]

In the postmodern era, poststructuralist theorists assert that there is a constructed cultural dimension to all materiality, and, hence, materiality becomes more and more open to human control. For example, hunger is no longer materially or naturally necessary, it is no longer outside human reach, but rather its form is actually culturally created. Social reality and social rhetoric are interwoven. Hunger is dependent on a human political decision. This is not meant to take away from or deny the material event of hunger, but rather to articulate it in a cultural and political arena wherein it can be seen as open to transformation.

A poststructuralist/post-Marxist reconceptualization of culture poses exciting political possibilities. Different aspects of capitalism can now be envisaged as fluid dimensions, which are upheld by certain political and cultural processes. As a result, the domain of politics becomes extended. Secondly, we can now conceptualize power in a different light. Power is now seen to be more visibly produced. It is more equally accessible, since it is an aspect of all cultural production, not just related to the cultural production by the dominant hegemony. Culture produces power, knowledge, identities, and ways of life. It therefore has the power to reshape social life. Because of the fluidity of the process of cultural production, social reconstruction is theoretically made possible. As a result, there can be strategic or ideological intervention into these processes aimed toward emancipatory political ends.

What does all this say to the matter in hand—developing a politics that speaks to the issue of early school-leaving? A poststructuralist/post-Marxist understanding of culture and cultural production can uncover the strategic limitations of the Marxist reproduction/resistance analysis of early school-leaving. Resistance theory—particularly as elaborated in the work of Paul Willis and as applied in this book in Chapter 5—investigates the importance of cultural processes. Willis analyzes cultural forms of resistance, but he concludes with the contradictory assessment that apparent resistance is nothing more than a cultural form of reproduction and that the resistance is a radical act in that it "refuses to collude in its own educational suppression" (Willis, 1977, p. 128). His work is informed by a Gramscian notion of hegemony, but because it is biased in favor of the force of reproductive powers it results in a view that resistance is merely a cultural process of reproduction.

The only way this contradiction can be resolved is by showing that while resistance does sometimes feed back into reproduction, it is always a fluid act that can be articulated in different ways. A cultural process cannot be read as a scientific or "objective rule." A cultural study need not always seek to uncover a stable format. The point of a "cultural study," as opposed to a "sociological study," is to investigate these processes in their fluid and contradictory wholeness rather than by identifying objective laws. Though cited as a cultural study, Willis's understanding of hegemony ensures that the resistance of "the lads" is over-determined by reproduction, albeit a "voluntary" form. In the reproduction/resistance analysis outlined in Chapter 5, the cultural production of the young people (in this case, their resistance) is repeatedly measured against a "classist" narrative within which the cultural production of resistance is not seen as important. In fact, the resistance analysis explicitly argues that cultural phenomena should be seen as politically inferior to class phenomena.

Within the resistance perspective, the young people's political criticisms of the educational system can be seen as something they would have been better off not to have realized, and their resistance to subordination as something they would have been better off not to have practiced. In the short term, their oppositional behavior is seen as non-emancipatory, violent, and angry. Rather than seeing this cultural process as a stepping-stone, it is seen as an end product. It is expected that their oppositional behavior could be emancipatory without any form of articulation or cultural strategy of intervention.

On the other hand, within a poststructuralist/post-Marxist understanding of cultural production, evidence of alternative forces of resistance can be interpreted as a starting point in the political struggle of early school-leavers. While resistance theory can further our understanding of these cultural processes, we must go beyond resistance theory because of the limitations it suffers from in relation to furthering a political project for early school-leavers. Even more important than providing a critique of reproduction/resistance theory, a poststructuralist/post-Marxist understanding of culture and cultural production is vital to the construction of early school-leavers as citizens with democratic rights which is seen as essential from a radical social democracy perspective.

Cultural studies can, in conclusion, be used to draw a picture of the political and cultural formation of the subject. It can be used, specifically, to show how the everyday lives of early school-leavers are constructed. In addition to this, a poststructuralist/post-Marxist concept of culture offers a basis for intervention strategies of political reconstruction. This conception of culture and cultural production provides us with understandings that expand our vision of the political domain of culture. The fluidity of the process of social construction is disclosed, empowering us to create new strategies of political intervention. Because culture is productive of power, knowledge, and social identities, there is room, through strategies of cultural production, to transform the forms of identification and constructions of subjectivity that currently exist into forms of identity with agency that are in keeping with the construction of radical democracy. However generalized and libertarian this may sound, in the particular case of early school-leavers this conceptualization of cultural production provides us with a basis from which to embark on a twofold strategy. First, it provides tools to move us beyond the political crisis of space experienced by early school-leavers through drawing up a cultural politics. Second, it points to the necessity of creating a cultural critical pedagogy that can intervene in the creation of negative social identities of young people who wish to leave school without educational qualifications.

NOTES

1. See the critique by N. Geras in "Post-Marxism?," *New Left Review*, *163* (May–June 1987) and the reply to the critique in E. Laclau, *New Reflections on the Revolution of Our Time* (London: Verso, 1991, pp. 97–134).

2. The argument in this paragraph is a synopsis of an argument presented by E. Laclau in *New Reflections* (1991, pp. 5–41).

3. See various histories of cultural studies; most cite its origins in the Birmingham Centre for Cultural Studies.

8

A Cultural and Pedagogical Politics of Early School-leaving

Foucault has suggested that talk of "radical" social change, of inventing new worlds, of transcending the world we live in, is in fact dangerous talk because it "has led only to the return of the most dangerous traditions" (Foucault, 1988, p. 46). The challenge of this work, then, is to construct a discourse of social change, but without transcending the realities of the everyday lives and struggles of the early school-leavers as they encounter them. The previous chapter has shown how some new movements and social theories have struggled with the problem of bringing about "partial transformations" without falling into global, essentialist, transcendental, and objectivist thought traps. In this spirit a cultural politics must be specific and partial while involved in a strategy for achieving a transformation of existing social relations. Political objectives cannot be overly specified in an a priori fashion where the dialectical quality of social life is lost in a totalizing strategy, but yet they cannot be totally absent since there is an ethical immediacy to uncovering the structural processes of victimization and blocking the creation of social victims.

In relation to the issue in hand in this book, direction can be derived from a political will to break through the current material and specific local space allocated to early school-leavers and to establish a new discursive political space. To broaden the establishment of more just social relations, the direction of this new cultural politics should draw not just from the specific issue of early school-leavers' subordination, but from a wider referent—that of broader democratic goals. However, the referent of radical democracy must be constantly confronted by the forces that affect the everyday existence of early school-leavers.

(RE)PRESENTING CULTURAL POLITICS

A cultural politics of early school-leaving is based on the understanding that culture produces power, knowledge, subjectivities, and identities; so, therefore, struggle at the cultural level is not only feasible but necessary. Cultural politics sets as its agenda the deliberate influencing of cultural forms of production—in other words, of what knowledges and identities are to be produced. Thus, in developing a cultural politics of early school-leaving the focus or objective is to influence the power relations, the knowledges, the identities, and subjectivities that are produced within the social relations of early school-leaving. Changing the knowledges and identities of early school-leavers involves learning and pedagogy, and influencing the power relations and subjectivities that are produced within relations of early school-leaving involves, in Tony Bennett's words, "talking to the Ideological State Apparatuses" (in Grossberg et al., 1992, p. 31). Central to this is the understanding that social relations are as culturally as they are economically produced, and that rhetoric, ideology, and the articulations of a more egalitarian vision of society are as "real," as "material," and in certain instances may be as effective in emancipatory transformation as are the most material of economic changes.

Can elements be drawn up of a provisional political strategy that avoids the dangerous totalitarian clarity of a reified end, that is not messianic but yet contains a strategy of cultural production? I wish to develop some directions for a cultural politics of early school-leaving, while being clearly aware of the dangers of constructing ritualized procedures or formulae. These directions will, hopefully, therefore seek to present an assemblage of representations of a lived engagement with the social world of early school-leavers. The engagement will be a politically sensitive one in that it critically examines how ideologies and identities are articulated into concrete social practices. These practices are seen by the early school-leavers as commonsensical and inevitable, but they are actually the mode through which the inequalities that affect them are constructed. At this point, in the context of this writing, I can discursively construct representations of points of departure for a cultural politics specific to the lived engagement of early school-leavers with their social world.

POINTS OF DEPARTURE

I consider the first point of departure for a cultural politics of early school-leaving to be the *identification of early school-leaving as one condition for establishing specific relations of subordination.* This is not to suggest that it is the only condition or that this condition is not caused by, or strongly related to, other factors. The factors involved in early school-leaving cross multiple lines of subjectivity, and the specificity of the relations of subordination will differ depending on how they are related to class, gender, race, and geographical location. I am not attempting here to cite early school-leaving as a founding moment or an original moment of suppression, to which all other forms of oppression can be related; rather, I am simply choosing early school-leaving as a specific moment to enter the cultural processes that bring about specific relations of subordination, and from this awareness to suggest an appropriate cultural politics.

Early school-leaving establishes particular relations of oppression that are not uniform or universal but are specific across gender, class, race, and geographical location. To escape speaking in universal terms, I wish to focus on the relations of subordination that are set up in relation to early school-leavers in one particular setting. I wish to speak specifically in terms of Irish early school-leavers. In outlining the specifics of their material location, we can identify early school-leaving as establishing particular relations of subordination in the Republic of Ireland.

The first three chapters of this book give cultural insight into "lived-in" relations of subordination. They provide representations of the lived, negotiated, and resisted everyday relations of subordination (financial, social, and work) that result from early school-leaving. The conversations on work or non-work situations disclose individual, rather than quantitative, accounts of the lived social relations of early school-leaving. The dialogues tell us that pay is experienced as a crucial and primary need of young people. Work that would keep them "off the streets" and "out of trouble" with the law (coming from highly policed geographical locations this is a serious consideration) is the most difficult thing to secure. The strongest form of subordination is reached when these young people feel that they cannot afford to imagine a long-term future. While these dialogues only record descriptions of recalled events, of episodes in the young people's lives, they do set a scene in which we can identify early school-leaving as one condition for establishing relations of subordination in that these early school-leavers do experience financial, work, and social status subordination.

To identify structurally that early school-leaving establishes relations of subordination in the Republic of Ireland, we need to turn to statistical accounts. Government reports give a statistical picture of the structural dimension of early school-leaving, of how many are affected, who is affected, and what the effects of early school-leaving are on the future social possibilities of early school-leavers. While I, for the moment, use this statistical approach, it is on the understanding that these are static and flat representations that falsely lay claim to an "objective" reality and thus can only be used with caution. They can be used further to constrain discursively early school-leavers in relations of subordination, or they can be used, as I wish to use them here, to describe statistically the material location of early school-leavers and to argue in ethical terms that this is an unacceptable situation that must be transformed.

Government reports in the 1980s draw a statistical picture of early school-leaving as a structural social problem.[1] They describe how Irish early school-leavers constitute almost 40% of the school-leaving cohort every year. Each year approximately five thousand students leave school with no qualifications, and they come almost exclusively from manual working-class backgrounds. Low participation rates in school correlate with a low position in the labor market, and, so, early school-leavers without any school qualifications face at best low-paid temporary work, without the possibility of advancement through training, or at worst long-term unemployment.[2] They are characterized as coming from economically disadvantaged backgrounds, with unemployment a general feature of their family background. Early school-leaving is portrayed very much as a class issue in the Irish context; gender appears as an issue, but not very significant statistically; race is not questioned, Ireland being made up of a fairly homogeneous population. These statistics "objectively" prove that, structurally, educational underachievement, nonparticipation in schooling, and early school-leaving place the early school-leavers in a subordinated position in that the possibility of their gaining access to further socioeconomic opportunity is greatly impaired. Relations of subordination are set up in that upon becoming early school-leavers they are placed in a lower socioeconomic stratum with the lowest financial income.

Despite the fact that these statistical accounts present a distorted, static, and flat representation, when taken up critically they can nevertheless provide valuable information. In the context of Ireland, statistical information confirms that early school-leaving and low participation rates set up chances where early school-leavers will be positioned in the lowest social stratum with the lowest financial income. (This does not negate the fact that this is also the background they are most likely to come from). They live a life in which their chances of employment are slim. If employed they are most likely to be engaged in unskilled labor that incorporates little or no training and few, if any, possibilities of advancement. In a work situation they will be positioned on the "bottom rung" of the hierarchy of authority. They are most likely to be engaged in short-term and part-time work, which is rarely a protected form of labor. The highest likelihood, however, is that they become either short-term or long-term dependents on social welfare; while it does set up some financial security for the early school-leaver (when old enough to become a recipient), it also serves to perpetuate relations of subordination associated with living below the established poverty line.

This statistical evidence of structured relations of subordination—combined with the representations of the "lived-in" everyday lives of the school-leavers presented in the earlier part of this book—can be used, on a preliminary basis, to identify early school-leaving as establishing relations of suppression, so as to convince the reader that early school-leavers occupy a material crisis of space. By this I mean to suggest that these relations of suppression have a material dimension to them that leaves the early school-leaver living in *an oppressive material location*.

The second element of a cultural politics of early school-leaving is the challenge *to delegitimate the current educational discursive construction around early school-leavers as victims*. Early school-leaving has traditionally been presented through a psychologistic discourse with a pathological aversion to politics, which has resulted in explanations that have to some extent been accepted in the larger society. Chapter 4 cites how academic educational discourses have historically blocked the politicization of the issue of early school-leaving. Genetic and cultural deprivation discourses can be challenged for their classist and racist formulations. They can also be critiqued for the deficit approach they take to the social experience, knowledge, subjectivity, and identity of early school-leavers. A cultural politics of early school-leaving would need to challenge strategically the classist, sexist, and racist underpinnings of these discourses which are supportive of a right-wing politics. What is made explicit in Chapter 4 is how these educational discourses are interested in maintaining the status quo by explaining structural inequalities as personal and cultural deficiencies. Reproduction and resistance theories can be examined in terms of the politics of how they situate the early school-leavers. How is the social experience, knowledge, subjectivity, and identity of early school-leavers theorized within these frameworks? Insofar as the early school-leaver is theorized as a non-agent and the discourse is closed to the possibility of transformation, these frameworks must be challenged because they construct the identity of the early school-leaver as that of victim.

A third necessary element of a cultural politics of early school-leaving would be *a grounding in the actual material terrain that early school-leavers occupy*, highlighting their struggle in terms of acknowledging the specificity of their demands, their concrete resistances, and their concrete struggle for a public sphere of influence. If we take as a sample the dialogue recorded in Part I and use it on a preliminary basis, we can glean from it suggestions on some characteristics of this material terrain and argue that it discloses a crisis of space.

In relation to schooling, their situation is that of exclusion. Their exclusion represents a "structural dislocation" generated by capitalism, and a corresponding social antagonism emerges. The early school-leavers' self-identity is in crisis. They clearly reject the identification offered them by the schooling system, which is that of being unintelligent and stupid. Early school-leavers often assume an identity that usually involves being able to "stand up for themselves." This form of identity is usually not accommodated within the schooling system and often becomes articulated by the schooling authorities negatively as "troublemaker." Yet for many early school-leavers it seems a more preferable type of identification. However, they are often forced out of school by the strength of the negative identification as "troublemakers," or they learn to escape from this stereotype by rejecting the institution they hold responsible for perpetrating relations of subordination. What results from this discrimination is a material crisis where early school-leavers are left without a positive identification in the domain of schooling. The inevitable result is that they are excluded from the educational system, excluded from qualifications, and sometimes reduced to searching for work without the necessary literacy and numeracy skills.

A material crisis of space is also apparent in relation to their work and future prospects. Underemployed or unable to obtain work, they find themselves in severe financial circumstances. The harsh reality of material poverty is something they have to deal with on an everyday basis. It involves restrictions such as being limited to one geographical terrain, to one or two types of leisure activity, to hanging about the home doing nothing but "going off the head," to harassment by the police, and eventually to taking risks at making money illegally.

What do they articulate as their demands? According to the dialogues recorded here, early school-leavers make particular demands on the schooling system. They desire an education that they feel is practical and appropriate to their needs. Because of their restricted material circumstances they primarily want an education that will obtain work for them. They want teachers who will not

"walk all over them" but who will treat them with respect; they
desire a schooling system that will take into account what type of
knowledge they have and want. In relation to work, their demands
center around obtaining employment—any employment. These
are old demands that have been negotiated many times before
by different social groups. However, a cultural politics of early
school-leavers must start from the point of being aware that these
are their most immediate demands and most immediate struggle.
Even though these are specific demands, however, this does not
mean that a cultural politics of early school-leaving is limited to
the direct or immediate taking up of these demands.

How can we read these dialogues as describing "identities in
culture"? It can be read that early school-leavers do struggle as
subjects; they exhibit historical agency in their continuous struggle which cannot be reduced to any founding moment. In relation
to school, they speak of moments of opposition, of resistance, of
the day they would finally take no more, or of the quiet continuous
resistance to schoolwork that they always considered was due to
"lack of interest". These oppositional stances are quite clear because they are what attracts attention given that resistance is the
form of struggle we can most easily grasp, both in terms of recognizing it in others and in practising it ourselves. Early school-
leavers do verbally and physically challenge what they see as
unacceptable points of subordination within the school. What is
not clear from these dialogues, because it was not directly queried
at the time of recording, is the extent to which these early school-
leavers move beyond resistance and inhabit new alternative ways
of being.

What we do know is that early school-leavers as subjects are
involved in an ongoing process of identification that encompasses
the movement from a negative identification to an attempt to set up
more positive forms of identity. They escape from the identification offered in their schooling and seek a more positive identification in the work sphere. It is at this point of their material crisis that
the process of identification is open to strategic intervention. If a
positive identification cannot be found in the workplace, then
other sites wherein an identity can be built are sought (e.g.,
parenting). Their identities will be split and diverse, but the immediacy of the material crisis still remains. Materially, they are situ-

ated in positions of dislocation. Within these positions, they are seeking to invent new subjectivities and identities that relate to their present material circumstances and struggles. At this point, it is necessary for early school-leavers that these social relations of subordination—which leave them unqualified, without work or an income—are articulated as relations of oppression. This would set a direction for forging new and more positive forms of identity. Understanding the material location of school-leavers can lead to positive interventions in their struggle for identity.

While an understanding of the material demands of early school-leavers is necessary as a basis for a cultural politics, these demands cannot totally dictate the political agenda. Their material struggle often articulates itself around socialist demands, despite the fact that the socialist project has, in the past, neglected many issues that play a part in their struggle. One example is the theorizing of gender relations. The new conceptualization of a cultural politics differs from traditional politics in that it operates simultaneously on two levels: first, it operates on the practical and local level of the struggle of early school-leavers; second, it must operate to provide a cultural vision of the construction of radical democracy. In operating on a practical and local level it must at one and the same time *be directed by an outside referent—namely, that of radical social democracy.* The duality of this political practice is the fourth point of departure of a cultural politics of early school-leaving.

The discourse of radical democracy can act as an external referent for their struggle and provide the articulation of the fact that their exclusion is a form of oppression. A key element in the strategy of radical democracy is the notion that specific democratic struggles require the expansion of what Laclau and Mouffe term "chains of equivalence," which extend and link them to other struggles. Dispersed democratic struggles can thus be seen as the raw material for broader popular struggles in specific conjunctures when there is a multiplication of equivalence effects among democratic struggles. Democratic struggles, including those of early school-leavers, are polysemic and can be articulated by very different discourses, as I argued in the Introduction. We must recognize crucially that it is through such articulations, and specifically their integration into a chain of equivalences, that these

struggles acquire their character. Given the current crisis of social
identities and the diverse interpellations to which they are subject,
early school-leavers' struggles need to recognize the chain of
equivalences that link them to other democratic struggles and the
equivalential articulation between, for example, antiracism, anti-
sexism, anticapitalism, and their own struggle.

The discourse of radical democracy can be used to negotiate the
particular demands of early school-leavers, in that it can alter these
demands to be as far-reaching as they are immediate. In being far-
reaching, greater support is lent to the struggle of early school-
leavers, which serves to open up a new cultural critical public
sphere and thus further the project of radical democracy. This discourse of radical democracy also aids the construction of early
school-leavers as social agents in that it offers more positive forms
of identification to the early school-leaver, who has historically
been excluded from the two major sources of social identification.
What this discourse achieves is that it moves the subjectivities of
early school-leavers from a reactive political position to a more
assertive and active political position.

The relationship between the concrete and local material struggles of early school-leavers and a cultural construction of radical
democracy could be of a new type: a relationship of negotiation
and movement. This should be an open-ended dialectical operation, in the sense that neither should attempt to bring the other to
closure, but both should be mutually informative. The material
demands of early school-leavers impact on the construction of
radical democracy, while at one and the same time the construction
of radical democracy reshapes their demands in certain ways.

Let me give an example of what kind of practice I am talking
about. The early school-leaver's primary demands for work and for
social status might need to be revised somewhat in response to the
new situations of structural unemployment experienced in late
capitalism and the demands this structural unemployment makes
on the political imagination. Rather than the politics of early
school-leaving being centered around a demand for work (which
would after all most probably entail vast exploitation of early
school-leavers in terms of the type of work that is deemed suitable
for them, e.g. government transition schemes), the idea of a radical
democratic imaginary suggests that the subordinate relations gen-

erated in such work environments along with the low and uncertain wages that they receive might be centered around alternative demands. It suggests that a redistribution of wealth might have to be rethought in an age of structural unemployment. In Ireland, unemployment rates are currently running as high as 20% (with 60% unemployed in some geographical areas). This is combined with massive youth emigration and government schemes that attempt to camouflage the extent of this structural unemployment. So, rather than early school-leavers struggling to attain work, they could be better served by demanding that the government respond more imaginatively to the overall situation of unemployment, by redistributing wealth in new ways and moving from the payment of subsistence money on social welfare to the payment of a viable income or a minimum wage.

Early school-leavers demand an education that is practical in terms of obtaining work, but, in the light of the above considerations, a cultural construction of a radical democracy suggests alterations on this demand. It suggests an education that teaches these young people their rights as democratic citizens, that empowers them to negotiate politically and produce strategies for community representation. This pedagogy would link their rights as democratic citizens to an understanding of their own specific struggle. The young people's demand that they be treated with respect by their teachers, that they be considered to have their own legitimate and worthwhile types of experiences, should be situated as a major entry point in the building of a cultural radical democratic politics of early school-leaving.

The fifth aspect of a strategic cultural politics of early school-leaving is the practice of a "communicative ethics," established between early school-leavers and those who acknowledge early school-leavers as people who are discursively unrepresented and who wish to work in solidarity with them. In this regard, Walsh argues that:

> Communicative ethics presupposes, and sustains, political transformation. The process of dialogue, mutual critique, and political action is dynamic, a spiralling movement in which rudimentary practises of political action enable further critique and evoke more adequate forms of political practice. [Welsh, 1991, p. 99]

In the case of early school-leavers, this is certainly necessary given that the nature of their subordination revolves around their exclusion from schooling and employment, and the fact that this exclusion is not named as such. For those who wish to work with early school-leavers, it is necessary to engage in a form of communicative ethics so as to become educated on the issue.

What exactly is involved in the practice of a communicative ethics, and what does it entail? The practice of a communicative ethics has been developed by Sharon Welsh,[3] who argues that

> morally transformative interaction requires far more than conversation between different groups and peoples, and that "genuine" conversation presupposes prior material interaction—either political conflict or coalition or joint involvement in life-sustaining work. [Welsh, 1991, p. 87]

Welsh believes that it is dangerous to assume that "one's own community and social class possess the pre-requisites for moral judgement and that other groups are devoid of those same pre-requisites" (Welsh, 1991, p. 87). When one is engaging in a communicative ethics, the cultural system and ethical standards of different types of communities will challenge each other, and the interaction between different groups will involve political coalitions along with an openness to political conflict. When we engage in a communicative ethics we learn about and acknowledge differences, and we are attentive to specific interests that must be dealt with rather than transcended. Within a communicative ethics there is a certain privilege given to the voice of the oppressed. Sharon Welsh refers to this as the epistemological privilege of the oppressed: "Those of us who are oppressed, while not having an ontologically given primacy, do have a point of view essential to moral critique" (Welsh, 1991, p. 90).

Sharon Welsh recognizes the possibility that there are interactions between groups in which power can be redistributed and social barriers removed. She theorizes the reconceptualization of new structures of thought and action that will enable this to happen and solidarity to be achieved. For Welsh, the first step is a "genuine conversation" or what I will refer to as dialogue. Gaining an education is a first condition of establishing this "genuine conversation." A second condition is that the intention of solidarity must be in operation during the dialogues.

> Solidarity has two aspects in this case: granting each group suffi-
> cient respect to listen to their ideas and to be challenged by them;
> recognition that the lives of the various groups are so intertwined
> that each is accountable to the other. These forms of recognition
> assume working together to bring about changes in social prac-
> tice. [Welsh, 1991, p. 95]

A dialogue can be transformative if those who wish to work with those who are more oppressed recognize the precariousness of the oppressive experience and become convinced that its human and social costs are intolerable. This could result in the attempt to eradicate all forms of injustice that affect others.

Welsh's notion of a communicative ethics involves addressing the notion of materiality at two points in the practice of this dia- logue. For Welsh, certain material conditions need to be met for a "genuine conversation" to happen. First, the number of people involved is important. Those experiencing the oppression should be numerically large enough to bring all the different points of view of that oppressed group to attention. Second, the material condition of equal weight being given in dialogue must be set up through examining the processes of the exclusion of the subordi- nated group.

In a communicative ethics of solidarity, mutual transformation can occur, but dialogue alone is not enough. A "genuine conversa- tion" that will result in mutual transformation can only be "the fruit of work together." By the term "working together," Sharon Welsh refers to the "material interaction at the most basic level" because one sees the physical effect required for sustenance and one can use this as a basis for a "genuine conversation."

If a communicative ethics of solidarity is a crucial element of a cultural politics of early school-leavers, how can this be practiced? First, gaining an education on the processes that affect early school-leaving is a condition for dialogue. If we want to use this book as a partial and specific model for the beginnings of a critical practice, we can find in Part I preliminary information that is a prerequisite for this dialogue with early school-leavers. It affords information that points to early school-leavers suffering from relations of subordination in terms of their exclusion from the educational process, the labor market, and the subsequent financial rewards. It holds information on the "commonsense" discourse that operates to pathologize early school-leavers and blocks these excluded people from being seen as fully human. It presents dialogues with early school-leavers, in which some of the conditions for a genuine conversation are present, representing an early attempt to establish a communicative ethics of solidarity.

A communicative ethics of solidarity is not quite reached here, even textually, because the major component of working together is not substantially present—a material interaction of working together with these young people. Given the form of the exclusion experienced by the early school-leavers, the work that I would see as being most appropriate and most useful would be to engage in a practice of critical cultural pedagogy. This, I argue, is an essential basis for a "genuine conversation" with early school-leavers and would incorporate practicing a communicative ethics of solidarity. Therefore, a *critical cultural pedagogy* is an essential aspect of, and for, a cultural politics specific to early school-leavers.

A CRITICAL CULTURAL PEDAGOGY
OF EARLY SCHOOL-LEAVERS

Two further moments of cultural production are required in the creation of a cultural politics of early school-leaving, both of which are related to pedagogy. The first is the creation of cultural workers who intend as their project to intervene both pedagogically and politically as cultural producers "to mobilize knowledge and desires that may lead to significant changes in minimizing the degree of oppression in people's lives" (Giroux & Trend, 1992, p. 32). The project for the construction of a new cultural politics and radical democracy necessitates a rethinking of the identity of the political activist. The role of the academic and organic intellectual is now being widely discussed in academic literature. New social movements have shown new ways of gaining political ground from the new types of activism practiced by feminism, gay and lesbian rights, and the black movement. The debates and achievements in these areas have contributed to the theorizing of the production and role of cultural workers.

I would describe a cultural worker as someone who sets as a personal goal the building of a cultural politics around the cultural work necessary for a radical democracy. Cultural workers act as political activists in the sense that they use a "language of critique and possibility that allows for multiple solidarities and political vocabularies while also articulating a common concern for extending the democratic principles of liberty, equality, and justice to the widest possible relations" (Giroux & Trend, 1992, p. 28). They also engage in a pedagogical practice as part of this cultural work to influence consciously the cultural production of meanings along with the construction of a more emancipatory form of community and everyday life. Cultural workers are engaged at two levels. First, there is a struggle to create new political spaces around the material crisis faced by early school-leavers, spaces that could articulate this material crisis as unjust and could at the same time feed into a more general and global discursive political formation of radical democracy. In this sense the term "cultural workers" can refer to those who wish to work in solidarity with early school-leavers, but it can also refer to early school-leavers who may take on the role of cultural worker.

Second, there is a pedagogical dimension to all cultural work and to the formation of a cultural politics. Intervention strategies of political and cultural reconstruction are implemented through these pedagogical practices. By pedagogical I refer to a process in the negotiation and production of meanings which takes into account the positioning within discursive practices of certain powers/knowledge relations (Giroux & McLaren, 1991, p. 157). However, the work of creating a cultural politics for, and of, early school-leavers demands the specific practicing of what I will refer to as a critical cultural pedagogy by early school-leavers.

By cultural critical pedagogy I mean to suggest a pedagogy that constitutes part of the cultural work of building a cultural politics. Critical pedagogy is a concept developed in the educational field which theorizes a form of education that leads to empowerment and is directed by, and implemented through, a vision of a democratic and just society. Following Giroux and McLaren:

> The term "critical pedagogy," by distinction, underscores the partisan nature of learning and struggle; it provides a starting point for linking knowledge to power and a commitment to developing forms of community life that take seriously the struggle for democracy and social justice. [Giroux & McLaren, 1991, p. 158]

While the early work on critical pedagogy is largely theorized within the educational system, the emphasis being on the direction and practice of an emancipatory schooling system, it is now beginning to be theorized as a form of cultural politics both inside and outside the educational system. Giroux describes how a critical pedagogy would act as a form of cultural politics:

> It draws attention to the ways in which knowledge, power, desire, and experience are produced under the basic conditions of learning. Both in and out of the academy this has meant a concern with analyses of the production and representation of meaning and how the practices they provoke are implicated in the dynamics of social power. [Giroux, 1992, pp. 239–240]

Giroux gives us the context in which critical pedagogy can operate as a form of cultural politics. He postulates critical pedagogy as a language of critique and possibility. In doing this, he moves into the terrain of a poststructural language that forms a basis for linking up with the discourse of cultural politics. He outlines three categories of discourse that link critical pedagogy with cultural politics; the discourse of production, the discourse of textual analysis, and the discourse of lived cultures (Giroux, 1988, pp. 132–146). Using these three theoretical categories I can describe what I mean by a specific cultural critical pedagogy of early school-leaving.

Working together in a pedagogical setting, cultural workers and early school-leavers could together attempt to reach an understanding of the social forces of production that operate outside that pedagogical setting to create culturally the process of their early school-leaving and their current material space. They learn from each other what the exact nature of these forces is. For example, a pedagogy that attempts to uncover the social forces of production that influence early school-leaving would ask questions like: is a system of gendering shaping the fact that young women are needed at home to do housework, or is it operating to produce early mothers? Is the economic system dictating that the family needs financial resources immediately as opposed to later? Is the community environment advocating that early school-leaving is profitable? Is there a structural process of selection at work in effect that is removing young people from school, and if so, why? In this book the structural forces are analyzed by those affected by them as a first step toward a social understanding of their position. However, the politics behind this investigation is a politics of human rights and human dignity. The pedagogical practice must not allow that this awareness limit or disempower; rather, it must ensure that these conditions are first understood so that they can be addressed as part of the political struggle.

The second category is that of textual analysis. In a classroom setting, this refers to a type of critique "capable of analyzing cultural forms as they are produced and used in specific classrooms" (Giroux, 1988, p. 138). A critical cultural pedagogy would critique and deconstruct texts in order to show how they are related to exclusions that in turn are related to early school-leaving and early school-leavers. However, within this discourse it is also possible for cultural workers and early school-leavers to use what they say about their early school-leaving, their work situation, or their future prospects as a specific text for them to interrogate and deconstruct. A pedagogy that could operate so as to deconstruct the text of what early school-leavers say about their social positioning (in terms of their material crisis of space) and the aim behind this pedagogy would be able to locate the contradictions in what they say so that new possibilities could emerge.

For example, in a pedagogical situation we could take the dialogues of Part I as a sample text they produced about their own lives. The cultural workers and early school-leavers could realize that the meaning produced in the text of what they say about their work situation is in direct contradiction to their resistant behavior. Contradiction could also be located in their descriptions of the depressing future prospects that they envisage for themselves and their present ability to struggle and enjoy life. In a pedagogy that practices the analysis of this text as a cultural form, these early

school-leavers could learn to visualize that they had actually produced meanings. The meanings and texts that early school-leavers
produce are not static entities, but can be re-read and reconstructed. This pedagogical textual analysis is very important to the
struggle of early school-leavers in that they must use certain critical tools to overview the text of their everyday lives and experiences and to search through these for moments of contradictions.
These contradictions can, through a practice of pedagogy, come to
be recognized by early school-leavers as moments of rupture and
of possibility. These can then serve as points from which early
school-leavers can begin to conceptualize and articulate their experiences as being political and thus begin to assert themselves as
agents in a political struggle.

Third, a cultural critical pedagogy operates within a discourse
of lived cultures or cultural life. While structural aspects of the
lives of early school-leavers have been examined under the rubrics
of a discourse of production, in this instance the pedagogy seeks to
analyze the subjective forms that early school-leavers inhabit. This
analysis assumes that lived experiences are not automatically determined by structural determinants. Therefore the early school-
leavers' lived-culture must be specifically dealt with as it becomes
a separate entity. At the level of this lived-culture there are elements of agency, determination, and self-production that can become evident through pedagogical procedures. In relation to early
school-leavers, it can be seen that they dropped out, in part,
through their own agency and self-production, along with their
mediation of certain social forces. Cultural workers and early
school-leavers can, through a pedagogy that concentrates on con-
firming and interrogating the experiential aspects of lived cultures,
investigate and take seriously the points of self-production and of
resistance as they are lived. These experiences are interrogated in
an effort to come to a better understanding of how power and
knowledge can empower the early school-leaver.

In general, a critical cultural pedagogy that supports a cultural
politics of early school-leaving would involve cultural workers
and early school-leavers working together in a pedagogical setting, in which they would analyze critically how cultural practices
relate to the current form of their everyday and community life.
This pedagogy would draw on the social imaginary of radical de-

mocracy to empower the early school-leavers and cultural workers to speak in terms of a better community life. There would be a search for strategies for achieving this. Together they would examine the specific contexts and constraints of the social and cultural practices that relate to their material location. In naming these practices and critically understanding them, there would be a search for moments of resistance and struggle where these points of resistance need to be articulated as points of power and as points for the formation of powerful identities.

For several reasons a critical cultural pedagogy is a central element of the radical politics being forged. The creation of a pedagogical context is necessary for working out the dynamics between the local material space of early school-leavers and the construction of a radical imaginary. The pedagogical dimension is part of an ongoing process of negotiation and dialogue that must work between these two elements of a cultural politics to bring about a new hegemonic politics. It has yet to be seen how far a critical pedagogy can go toward working out these specific political objectives. However, in the first instance it must work as an interrogatory form of negotiation in the construction of meanings and knowledge. This negotiation, in the process of its discussion, actually performs a role in the production of identities.

Second, the cultural politics of early school-leavers is not just about taking the local material crisis of early school-leaving and moving on to theorize a new politics, but is also about the early school-leavers as people. In a very concrete way, cultural politics is about working with people, not just the theoretical dimensions that are manifested in their politics, identities, subjectivities, and knowledge. As mentioned earlier, a cultural politics linked with a communicative ethics of solidarity rests on the basis of shared work. The main type of constructive and necessary work that can be shared by, and with, early school-leavers and cultural workers is the practice of a critical pedagogy. The cultural politics of early school-leaving involves a responsibility on the part of early school-leavers and cultural workers to engage in a pedagogical practice with each other. Because early school-leavers have been excluded to such an extent, having resisted school they now have a vested interest in the production of knowledge that will engage their experiences critically in terms of the existing power and knowledge relations. A pedagogical setting is necessary for the young people to have the freedom to speak in an environment where they can develop their thoughts in relation to possible political strategies as opposed to having to take an immediate stance of resistance to protect themselves. This involves creating pedagogical sites of interaction where people engage in the praxis of productive pedagogy.

The cultural politics of early school-leaving is about transformation and the creation of new political possibilities, on both a local and a global level. However, it is very important to understand the specificity of the cultural politics outlined here. At no level is there, or should there be, an attempt to universalize the experience of these early school-leavers. The dimensions of early school-leaving as they appear in this text describe a specific Irish context. In writing a cultural politics of early school-leaving I am not attempting to set up a master narrative of struggle but merely wish to set up specific strategies for this context.

This book is written in order to play a role in the struggle to create a new political space around the issue of early school-leaving. To do this, it has attempted to play a concrete role in creating a cultural politics of early school-leaving. The theoretical creation of this cultural politics has been written here, but this writing also contains many practical, activist, and political manoeuvres. Yet the cultural politics is not complete. It is not complete because it should not be complete, but continuously open as a process of its own theory and practice. The political struggle for transformation can afford neither theoretical nor practical closure.

NOTES

1. See government social research work on the statistical dimension to early school-leaving produced in the 1980s which uncovers the structuring of educational underachievement in Ireland. In particular, see R. Breen, *Education and the Labour Market* (1984a); R. Breen et al., *School Leavers 1980– 1986* (1986); and J. J. Sexton, *Transition from School to Work* (1988).

2. In Ireland this constitutes living well below the poverty line: see *Combat Poverty: Annual Report 1987* (Dublin: Combat Poverty Agency, 1987).

3. Sharon Welsh develops this notion of communicative ethics in response to Habermas's well-known project of communicative competency and his model for undistorted communications. She rejects the politics of consensus, which, she argues, is part of Habermas's project. For a summary and further commentary on this debate see P. McLaren, "Post-Modernism, Post-Colonialism and Pedagogy," in *Education and Society*, *9* (No. 1, 1991), 3–22. For extended discussion on a radical politics of ethics dialogue and pedagogy see H. Giroux, *Schooling and the Struggle for Public Life* (Minneapolis, MN: University of Minnesota Press, 1988).

REFERENCES AND BIBLIOGRAPHY

Apple, M. (1979). *Ideology and Curriculum.* London: Routledge & Kegan Paul.

Apple, M. (1982a). *Culture and Economic Reproduction in Education.* London: Routledge & Kegan Paul.

Apple, M. (Ed.) (1982b). *Education and Power.* Boston, MA: Routledge & Kegan Paul.

Aronowitz, S. (1986/87). "Theory and Socialist Strategy." *Social Text* (No. 16, Winter), 1–16.

Aronowitz, S. (1981). *The Crises in Historical Materialism: Class, Politics, and Culture in Marxist Theory* (2nd edition). Minneapolis, MN: University of Minnesota Press, 1991.

Aronowitz, S., & Giroux, H. (1986). *Education under Siege: The Conservative, Liberal and Radical Debate over Schooling.* London: Routledge & Kegan Paul.

Aronowitz, S., & Giroux, H. (1991). *Postmodern Education: Politics, Culture and Social Criticism.* Minneapolis, MN: University of Minnesota Press.

Arnot, M., & Whitty, G. (1982). "School Texts, The Hidden Curriculum and The Curriculum in Use: A British view of Recent American Contribution to the Sociology of the Curriculum." *Discourse, 3* (No. 1), 1–12.

Atkinson, P. (1990). *The Ethnographic Imagination*. London: Routledge.

Bennett, T., Mercer, C., & Wolacott, J. (1986). *Popular Culture and Social Relations*. Milton Keynes, U.K.: Open University Press.

Bernstein, B. (1971). *Class, Codes and Control*. London: Routledge & Kegan Paul.

Bernstein, B. (1985). "A Socio-Linguistics Approach to Social Learning." In: *Penguin Survey of the Social Sciences*, edited by J. Gould. Harmondsworth, U.K.: Penguin.

Berwick, P., & Burns, M. (Eds.) (1982). *Conference on Poverty*. Dublin: The Council for Social Welfare.

Bhabha, Homi. (1988). "The Commitment to Theory." *New Formations*, 5 (Summer), 5–22.

Bhavnani, K. (1991). *Talking Politics, A Psychological Framing for Views from Youth in Britain*. Cambridge, U.K.: Cambridge University Press.

Blackledge, D., & Hunt, Q. (1985). *Sociological Interpretations of Education*. London: Croom Helm.

Bobbio, N. (1976). *Which Socialism? Marxism, Socialism, and Democracy*, translated by Roger Griffin, edited and introduced by Richard Bellamy. Minneapolis, MN: University of Minnesota Press, 1987.

Bobbio, N. (1990). *Liberalism and Democracy*, translated by Martin Ryle & Kate Soper. London: Verso.

Bourdieu, P. (1976). "Systems of Education and Systems of Thought." In: *Schooling and Capitalism*, edited by R. Dale et al. London: Routledge & Kegan Paul.

Bourdieu, P., & Passeron. J. G. (1977). *Reproduction in Education, Society and Culture*. London: Sage.

Bowles, S., & Gintis, H. (1976). *Schooling in Capitalist America*. London: Routledge & Kegan Paul.

Breen, R. (1984a). *Education and the Labour Market: Work and Unemployment among Recent Cohorts of Irish School-Leavers*. Dublin: Economic and Social Research Institute, Paper 119.

Breen, R. (1984b). "Status Attainment or Job Attainment? The Effects of Sex and Class on Youth Unemployment." *British Journal of Sociology, 35* (No. 3), 363–386.

Breen, R. (1991). *Education, Employment and Training in the Youth Labour Market*. Dublin: Economic and Social Research Institute.

Breen, R., Whelan, B., & Costigan, J. (1986). *School Leavers 1980–1986. A Report to the Department of Labour*. Dublin: Economic and Social Research Institute.

Clancy, P. (1982). *Participation in Higher Education*. Dublin: The Higher Education Authority.

Clark, L. (1982). *The Transition from School to Work: A Critical Review of Research in the United Kingdom*. London: HMSO.

Clifford, J. (1983). "On Ethnographic Authority." *Representations, 1* (No. 2), 69–73.

Clifford, J. (1986). "Introduction: Partial Truths." In: J. Clifford & G. Marcus, *Writing Culture: The Politics and Poetics of Ethnography* (Berkeley, Los Angeles, and London: University of California Press).

Clifford, J. (1988). *The Predicament of Culture: Twentieth Century Ethnography and Literature*. Cambridge, MA: Harvard University Press.

Combat Poverty Agency (1987). *Combat Poverty: Annual Report 1987*. Dublin.

Corrigan, P. (1979). *Schooling and the Smash Street Kids*. London: MacMillan.

Crooks, T., & Stokes, D. (Eds.) (1987). *Disadvantage, Learning and Young People*. Dublin: CDVEC Curriculum Unit.

Cullen, M. (Ed.) (1987). *Girls Don't Do Honours—Irish Women in Education in the 19th and 20th Centuries*. Dublin: Women's Education Bureau.

Danaher, G., Frain, P., & Sexton, J. (1985). *Manpower Policy in Ireland*. Dublin: The National Economic and Social Council, NESC Report No. 82.

Dean, J. P. (1954). "The Method of Unstructured Pilot Enquiry." In: *An Introduction of Social Research*, edited by J. T. Doby. London: Stackpole.

Delamont, S. (1983). *Interaction in the Classroom*. London: Methuen.

Delamont, S. (Ed.) (1984). *Reading on Interaction in the Classroom*. London: Methuen.

Everhart, R. (1983). *Reading, Writing and Resistance*. London: Routledge & Kegan Paul.

Fagan, H. (1989). *Resisting School: The Educational Experience of Irish Early School-Leavers from Lower Socio-Economic Background* (unpublished). St. Patrick's College, Maynooth, Ireland.

FAS (1988). *Beyond School*. Dublin: CDVEC, Curriculum Development Unit.

FAS (1989a). *YouthReach: Operators' Guideline—Draft.* Dublin: YouthReach Working Group.

FAS (1989b). *YouthReach: A Summary.* Dublin: YouthReach Working Group.

Feldstein, M., & Elwood, D. (1982). "Teenage Unemployment: What Is the Problem?" In: *The Youth Labour Market, Its Nature, Causes and Consequences,* edited by Freeman & Wise. Chicago, IL: National Bureau of Economic Research.

Fine, M. (1991). *Framing Dropouts*: New York: Suny Press.

Flew, A. (1976). *Sociology, Equality and Education.* London: Macmillan.

Foucault, M. (1979). *The History of Sexuality, Vol. 1: An Introduction.* London: Allen Lane.

Foucault, M. (1980). *Power, Knowledge: Selected Interviews and Other Writings 1972–77,* edited by Colin Gordon. New York: Pantheon.

Foucault, M. (1988). *Politics, Philosophy, Culture: Interviews and Other Writings 1977–84,* edited with an introduction by Lawrence D. Kritzman. New York: Routledge.

Fraser, N. (1989). *Unruly Practices: Power, Discourse and Gender Contemporary Social Theory.* Minneapolis, MN: University of Minnesota Press.

Freire, P. (1972). *Pedagogy of the Oppressed.* Harmondsworth, U.K.: Penguin.

Galton, F. (1869). *Hereditary Genius.* London: Macmillan, 1969.

Game, A. (1991). *Undoing the Social, Toward a Deconstructive Sociology.* Milton Keynes, U.K.: Open University Press.

Geary, R. C., & Hughes, J. G. (1970). *Internal Migration in Ireland.* Dublin: Economic and Social Research Institute, Paper No. 55.

Giroux, H. (1983a). "Theories of Reproduction and Resistance in the New Sociology of Education: A Critical Analysis." *Harvard Educational Review, 53* (No. 3), 257–293.

Giroux, H. (1983b). *Theory and Resistance in Education: A Pedagogy for the Opposition.* London: Heinemann Educational Books.

Giroux, H. (1988). *Schooling and the Struggle for Public Life: Critical Pedagogy in the Modern Age.* Minneapolis, MN: University of Minnesota Press.

Giroux, H. (1992). *Border Crossings: Cultural Workers and the Politics of Education.* New York: Routledge.

Giroux, H., & McLaren, P. (1990). "Language, Schooling, and Subjectivity: Beyond a Pedagogy of Reproduction and Resistance."

In: *Contemporary Issues in U.S. Education*, edited by Kathryn Borman et al. New York: Ablex.

Giroux, H., & McLaren, P. (1991). "Radical Pedagogy as Cultural Politics: Beyond the Discourse of Critique and Anti-Utopianism." In: *Texts for Change: Theory/Pedagogy/Politics*, edited by Donald Morton & Mas'ud Zavarzadeh. Urbana, IL: University of Illinois Press.

Giroux, H., & Trend, D. (1992). "Cultural Workers, Pedagogy, and the Politics of Difference: Beyond Cultural Conservatism." In: H. Giroux, *Border Crossings: Cultural Workers and the Politics of Education*. New York: Routledge.

Goodwin, L (1970). *Do the Poor Want To Work*. London: Brookings Institute.

Goodwin, L. (1972). "How Suburban Families View the Work Orientations of the Welfare Poor." *Social Problems, 19* (No. 3), 50–72.

Gould, J. (Ed.) (1985). *Penguin Survey of the Social Sciences*. Harmondsworth, U.K.: Penguin.

Gramsci, A (1971). *Selections from the Prison Notebooks*. New York: International Publishers.

Gramsci, A. (1978). *Selections from Political Writings of Antonio Gramsci*, edited by Quintin Hoare. London: Lawrence & Wishart.

Gramsci, A. (1985). *Selections from Cultural Writings*, edited by David Forgacs & Geoffrey Nowell-Smith. London: Lawrence & Wishart.

Grossberg, L., Nelson, C., & Treichler, P. (1992). *Cultural Studies*. New York: Routledge.

Hannan, D., Breen, R., Murray, B., Watson, D., Hardiman, N., & O'Higgins, K. (1983). *Schooling and Sex-Roles: Sex Difference and Student Choice in Irish Post-Primary Schools*. Dublin: Economic and Social Research Institute, Paper No. 113.

Hargreaves, A. (1982). "Resistance and Relative Autonomy Theories: Problems of Distortion and Incoherence in Recent Marxist Analysis of Education." *British Journal of Sociology of Education, 3* (No. 2), 107–126.

Hickox, M. S. H (1982). "The Marxist Sociology of Education: A critique." *The British Journal of Sociology, 33* (No. 4), 563–577.

Hollands, R. G. (1990). *The Long Transition: Class, Culture, and Youth Training*. London: Macmillan Education.

Holman, R. (1978). *Poverty: Explanations of Social Deprivation*. London: Martin Robinson.

Jackson, P. (1984). "Training Schemes—A Dilemma for Community Work in Ireland." *Community Development Journal*, 19 (No. 2), 82–87.

Jameson, F. (1981). *The Political Unconscious: Narrative as a Socially Symbolic Act*. New York: Cornell University Press.

Keddie, N. (1973). *Tinker, Tailor, Soldier, Sailor: The Myth of Cultural Deprivation*. Harmondsworth, U.K.: Penguin.

Kellaghan, T., & Greaney, V. (1984). *Equality of Opportunity in Irish Schools*. Dublin: The Educational Company.

Laclau, E. (1991). *New Reflections on the Revolution of Our Time*. London: Verso.

Laclau, E., & Mouffe, C. (1985). *Hegemony and Socialist Strategy*. London: Verso.

Lawton, D. (1975). *Clan, Culture and the Curriculum*. London: Routledge & Kegan Paul.

Lovin, R. W., & Perry, J. (1990). *Critique and Construction—A Symposium on Roberto Unger's Politics*. Cambridge: Cambridge University Press.

McGreil, M. (1974). *Educational Opportunity in Dublin*. Dublin: The Research and Development Unit.

McHunt, J. (1970). "Poverty Versus Equality of Opportunity." In: *Psychological Factors in Poverty*, edited by V. Allen. London: Markham.

McLaren, P. (1986). *Schooling as a Ritual Performance*. London: Routledge & Kegan Paul.

McLaren, P. (1989). *Life in Schools: An Introduction to Critical Pedagogy in the Foundations of Education*. New York: Longman.

McLaren, P. (1991). "Post-Modernism, Post-Colonialism and Pedagogy." *Education and Society, 9* (No. 1), 3–22.

McRobbie, A. (1980). "Settling Accounts with Subcultures: A Feminist Critique." *Screen Education* (No. 34, Spring), 37–49.

McRobbie, A. (1992). "Post-Marxism and Cultural Studies: A Postscript." In: *Cultural Studies* (pp. 719–731), edited by L. Grossberg, C. Nelson, & P. Treichler. New York: Routledge.

McRobbie, A., & Garber, J. (1976). "Girls and Subcultures." In: *Resistance through Ritual*, edited by S. Hall & T. Jefferson. London: Hutchinson.

Mouffe, C. (1988a). "Hegemony and New Political Subjects: Toward a New Concept of Democracy." In: *Marxism and the Interpreta-*

tion of Culture (pp. 89–105), edited by Cary Nelson & Larry Grossberg. Urbana, IL: University of Illinois Press.

Mouffe, C. (1988b). "Radical Democracy: Modern or Postmodern." In: *Universal Abandon: The Politics of Postmodernism*, edited by A. Ross. Minneapolis, MN: University of Minnesota Press.

Mouffe, C. (1988c). "Rawls: Political Philosophy without Politics." *Philosophy and Social Criticism, 13* (No. 2), 105–123.

Mouffe, C. (1989). "Toward a Radical Democratic Citizenship." *Democratic Left, 17* (No. 2), 6–7.

National Economic & Social Council (1985). *Manpower Policy in Ireland*. NESC Report No. 84. Dublin.

National Economic and Social Council (1991). *The Economic and Social Implications of Emigration*. Dublin.

National Economic and Social Council (1992). *The Association Between Economic Growth and Employment Growth in Ireland*. Dublin.

National Economic and Social Council (1993). *Education and Training Policies for Economic and Social Development*. Dublin.

Oakes, J. (1982). "Classroom Social Relationships: Exploring the Bowles and Gintis Hypothesis." *Sociology of Education, 55* (October), 197–212.

O'Cinneide, S. (1985). "Community Response to Unemployment." *Administration* (No. 2), 231–257.

Passon, A., & Elliot, D. (1968). "The Nature and Needs of the Educationally Disadvantaged." In: *Developing Programmes for the Educationally Disadvantaged*, edited by A. Passon. New York: Teachers College Press.

Pavalko, R. (Ed.) (1970). *Sociology of Education: A Book of Readings*. Chicago, IL: F. E. Peacock.

Postman, N., & Weingartner, C. (1969). *Teaching as a Subversive Activity*. Harmondsworth, U.K.: Penguin.

Robinson, P. (1976). *Education and Poverty*. London, Methuen.

Ronayne, T. (1986). *The Living Conditions of the Long Term Unemployed: Case Studies of Innovations*. Dublin: Irish Foundation for Human Development.

Rose, H., & Rose, S. (1979). "The IQ Myth." In: *Education and Equality*, edited by D. Rubenstein. Harmondsworth, U.K.: Penguin.

Rottman, D. B. (1982). *The Distribution of Income in the Republic of Ireland: A Study in Social Class and Family Cycle Inequalities*. Dublin: Economic and Social Research Institute, Paper No. 109.

Rubenstein, D. (Ed.) (1979). *Education and Equality*. Harmondsworth, U.K.: Penguin.

Rubenstein, D., & Stoneman, L. (1970). *Education and Democracy*. Harmondsworth, U.K.: Penguin.

Ryan, M. (1989). *Politics and Culture: Working Hypotheses for a Post-Revolutionary Society*. Baltimore, MD: The Johns Hopkins Press.

Sarup, M. (1982). *Education, State and Crisis*. London: Routledge & Kegan Paul.

Selltiz, C. (1976). *Research Methods in Social Relations*. New York: Holt, Reinhart & Wilson.

Sexton, J. J. (1988). *Transition from School to Work and Early Labour Market Experience*. Dublin: Economic and Social Research Institute, Paper No. 141.

Sherman, E. (1967). *Evaluative Research*. New York: Russell Sage Foundation.

Stephanson, A. (1988). "Regarding Postmodernism: A Conversation with Fredric Jameson." In: *Universal Abandon?: The Politics of Postmodernism* (pp. 3–30), edited by Andrew Ross. Minneapolis, MN: University of Minnesota Press.

Strategies Collective (1988). "Building A New Left: An Interview with Ernesto Laclau." *Strategies* (Fall), 10–28.

Swan, L. D. (1978). *Reading Standards in Irish Schools*. Dublin: The Educational Company of Ireland.

Turner, G. (1990). *British Cultural Studies, An Introduction*. London: Unwin & Hyman.

Tyler, W. (1977). *The Sociology of Educational Inequality*. London: Methuen.

Unger, R. M. (1987). *Politics, A Work in Constructive Social Theory, Vol. I: False Necessity, Anti-Necessitarian Social Theory in the Service of Radical Democracy*. Cambridge: Cambridge University Press.

Walker, R. (Ed.) (1985). *Applied Quantitative Research*. Brookfield, IL: Gower.

Welsh, S. (1985). *Communities of Resistance and Solidarity: A Feminist Theology of Liberation*. New York: Orbis Books.

Welsh, S. (1991). "An Ethics of Solidarity and Difference." In: *Postmodernism, Feminism and Cultural Politics: Redrawing Educational Boundaries*, edited by Henry Giroux. New York: SUNY Press.

Whelan, C. T. (1980). *Employment Condition and Job Satisfaction:*

The Distortion, Perception and Evaluation of Job Rewards. Dublin: Economic and Social Research Institute, Paper No. 101.

Whelan, C. I. (1983). *Survey of Youth Unemployment and the Transition from Education to Working Life.* Dublin. Economic and Social Research Institute, Report to the EEC Commission.

Whitty, G., & Young, M. (Eds.) (1977). *Society, State and Schooling.* Lewes: Falmer Press,

Willis, P. (1977). *Learning to Labour.* Farnborough, U.K.: Saxon House.

Willis, P. (1983). "Cultural Production and Theories of Reproduction." In: *Race, Class and Education,* edited by L. Bourbon & S. Walther. London: Croom Helm.

Wilson, H. (1970). "The Socialization of Children." In: *Socially Deprived Families in Britain.* London: Bedford Square Press.

Woods, P. (Ed.) (1980a). *Pupil Strategies.* London: Croom Helm.

Woods, P. (Ed.) (1980b). *Teacher Strategies.* London: Croom Helm.

Young, M. F. D. (1971). *Knowledge and Control: New Direction for the Sociology of Education.* London: Collier–MacMillan.

Youth Employment Agency (1983). *Youth Employment Levy: A Review of Activities Supported and Their Impact in 1983.* Dublin.

Youth Employment Agency (1984). *A Social Guarantee for Young People.* Dublin.

Youth Employment Agency (1985). *Youth Employment Levy: A Review of Activities Supported and Their Impact in 1985.* Dublin.

Youth Employment Agency (1986). *Report on the First Year of Implementation of the Social Guarantee for Young People.* Dublin.

Youth Employment Agency (1987). *Report on the Second Year of the Implementation of the Social Guarantee for Young People.* Dublin.

INDEX

181

ABOUT THE AUTHOR

G. HONOR FAGAN, a native of Ireland, completed her graduate studies in education at the University of Miami in Ohio. After leaving her lecturing post in sociology at the University of Ulster, she took her present position as sociology lecturer at the University of Durban-Westville in South Africa. She is the coeditor of *Gendered Narratives, Aspects of Cultural Identity in Ireland* (1995).

ISBN 0-89789-439-1

HARDCOVER BAR CODE